Stratégie

Stratégie

Business Intelligence & Analytics

Dr. Anupama Rajesh
Havish Madhvapaty
Vatsal Sahani

PARTRIDGE

To order additional copies of this book, contact
Partridge India
000 800 10062 62
orders.india@partridgepublishing.com

www.partridgepublishing.com/india

TABLE OF CONTENTS

MARKETING ANALYTICS
Prateek Mangal

MARKETING ANALYTICS: CASES
Kritika Nagdev

SECTION: FINANCIAL ANALYTICS

FINANCIAL ANALYTICS
Vatsal Sahani

FINANCIAL ANALYTICS USING EVIEWS
Parul Kumar

IBM SPSS
Havish Madhvapaty

R (PROGRAMMING LANGUAGE)
Vipul Pandey

PREFACE

Ubiquitous digitization and connectivity has brought a significant shift in the functioning of organisations. Often the problem is not in the collection of data but to "make sense" of it.

To combat globalized competition, enterprises strive to create a differentiated position for themselves. They require the support of extensive data processing and analytical techniques to bolster their processes. New tools and techniques are required consistently to support and empower decision-making capabilities. Hence, there has been a phenomenal rise in decision support technologies of which Business Intelligence and Analytics (BI&A) form a substantial part.

IBM Tech Trends Reports have for consecutive years identified Business Intelligence and Analytics as one of the leading technological trends. Research by Gartner (world's leading IT research firm) also states that BI&A is one of the top most priority technology investments.

The book "STRATÉGIE: Business Intelligence & Analytics" comes at an opportune time to provide a holistic overview of this very significant technology. The introductory chapter discusses Business Intelligence and Analytics and various associated concepts, components, infrastructure etc. in detail. The subsequent chapters deal with BI&A in various verticals of management such as Marketing, Human Resources, Finance etc.

Marketing analytics is the practice of collecting, managing, measuring and analyzing marketing performance of an organization through certain processes and technologies. Marketing analytics chapter introduces core concepts to the readers giving them working knowledge and understanding of the topic. The readers will also gain by learning the concept of customer analytics and its most relevant techniques used by companies around the world. The techniques are elaborated and explained by way of sample examples for understanding consumer insights and application for market segmentation and positioning.

Financial analytics is the art of putting together data in a derivative and comprehensible view from a large set of financial data to aid decision making. The section on financial analytics discusses key concepts as well as tools used such as econometric modeling, time series, regression analysis etc.

HR analytics simplifies critical human resource challenges and makes the function more quantitative rather than qualitative. The chapter on HR analytics details associated concepts taking examples from the business world. It also discusses the statistical tools most relevant to HR.

Prevalent analytical software is also discussed and their options detailed in an easy-to-understand manner. Excel and SPSS are the most widely used spreadsheet and statistical software respectively. Excel is a very powerful tool to collate and analyze data. The chapter on Excel serves to demystify these capabilities for the user who intends to leverage from Excel's diverse tools. The chapter on SPSS covers the core essentials of the most relevant tools.

R is an open source software providing a low- cost alternative to expensive proprietary software. It has a command language for various statistical techniques. The chapter deals with its more important features.

This book is, therefore, a comprehensive treatise of analytics basics, software and applications. It aims at providing useful knowledge to students, instructors and practitioners alike.

This book is a result of the best wishes and blessings of my family & friends and above all the Almighty.

Dr. Anupama Rajesh

DATA MUST INDEED TELL A STORY BUSINESS INTELLIGENCE: THE INTELLIGENT WAY OF DOING BUSINESS

AUTHOR BIO

Dr. Anupama Rajesh

Dr. Anupama Rajesh is Professor at Amity Business School, Amity University, India. She has a teaching experience of over 20 years including international assignments which include a teaching stint in London and Singapore and training of Italian and French delegates and students. She has been trained for Case Writing at INSEAD Paris, and has written more than 40 research papers and case studies for prestigious international journals and has eight books and several book chapters to her credit. She is reviewer of renowned Sage and Emerald journals. Her research interests are Business Intelligence, Educational Technology, Marketing Analytics etc. while her teaching interests are Business Intelligence, E-Commerce, IT enabled processes and so on.

She is an avid trainer and has trained Union Bank of India, NHPC, ILFS, TATA Motors, Bhutan Power Company employees as well as Commonwealth Games Volunteers and army personnel. She is a Master Trainer from Microsoft, Infosys Partner for Business Intelligence and Academic Partner for SAP ERM Sim.

She has recently won the ADMA Research Award. She has also been awarded "Shiksha Rattan Puruskar" and won several Outstanding Paper Awards at prestigious conferences at institutes such as IIM Ahmedabad. She also has a MOOC to her credit.

1. INTRODUCTION

Ubiquitous digitization and connectivity has brought a significant shift in the functioning of organisations. Increasingly data is being "born digital". At times organisations are faced with deluge of data and cases of "data overload". Often the problem is not in the collection of data but to "make sense" of it.

To combat globalized competition, enterprises strive to create a differentiated position for themselves. They require the support of extensive data processing and analytical techniques to bolster their processes. New tools and techniques are required consistently to support and empower decision-making capabilities. Hence there has been a phenomenal rise in decision support technologies of which Business Intelligence and Analytics (BI&A) form a substantial part.

IBM Tech Trends Reports have for consecutive years identified Business Intelligence and Analytics (BI&A) as one of the leading technological trends. Research by Gartner (World's leading IT research firm) also states that BI&A is one of the top most priority technology investments. This exponential growth of each aspect of these technologies may also be attributed to a sharp decline in the costs of collection and storage of large amounts of data of all aspects of business – for example customer data, inventory data, logistics data, social media data. Associated low connectivity costs have further fuelled this growth. Self-service models of implementation are further catalysing its implementation. User-friendly interfaces such as drag and drop, and point and click functionalities are adding to their popularity. These empower users to perform different analytical operations as per their own requirements without the interventions of the IT department / personnel.

Business Intelligence has always been used as an encompassing terminology for all processes, tools, applications and technologies which can be used for collecting, storing, organising, analysing and reporting data. Hence it is also referenced as Business Intelligence and Analytics (BI&A). It helps to gain useful insights into all kinds of enterprise, customer, user, product data. These then become valuable inputs to better and quicker decision making. With increased pressures of competition on enterprises, and resultant need for agility – almost real-time analytics is required – where the time lag between data collection and analysis is reduced significantly.

2. THE EVOLUTION

BI&A will always be associated with Data Management. Business Intelligence has had a distinct evolution since 1990s, when it was first introduced by Business and IT communities. The term "BI" was first coined by IBM researcher Hans Peter Luhn in 1958, who defined intelligence as "ability to apprehend the inter-relationships of presented facts in such a way as to guide action towards a desired goal". It gained popularity due to Gartner Analyst Howard J Dresner who described BI, in 1989, as "a set of concepts and methods to improve business decision making by using fact based support system".

Analytics was given a special mention by Davenport in their very popular book "Competing by Analytics". BI&A in its earliest avatar relied largely on structured data stored in Relational Databases obtained from various operational databases across the enterprise. With the advent of Big Data (used to refer to very large and complex datasets of company, sensor, mobile and web data), it is often such kinds of enormous collections of data which are being used for intelligence and analytics.

A. BI&A 1.0

This refers to initial techniques of collecting, extracting and analysing data. Data collected from operational as well as legacy databases was structured and usually relational, hence easy to extract and load into data warehouses. The tools used were basic such as simple querying, online analytical querying (OLAP), reporting and graphics. Business Process Management (BPM) was suitably aided by metrics and visualizations. Data mining tools helped in association, segmentation, clustering, classification analysis as well as predictive techniques. Exception and anomaly detection were also key implements. Loading key result areas into easily accessible and interpretable dashboards was another very useful feature.

Of the 13 elements of the present day BI platforms, as per a Gartner report by Sallam et al., following have been mentioned as BI&A 1.0: reporting, ad hoc queries, search based BI, visualizations, dashboards, scorecards, data mining and predictive modelling.

B. BI&A 2.0

In the next few years it was observed that it was not sufficient to have one sided interactions with stakeholders as in Web 1.0. There was a constant need for exchange of information. The users were increasingly interacting with the web and there was an increased need to "listen" to one's customers. The content generated did not always conform to inflexible Relational Database products. Search, interactions, cookies etc. were a treasure house of information of users and gave valuable insights. Search history, web logs etc. supplemented by cookies and server data was divulging meaningful patterns of user needs and opened flood gates of various opportunities. Customer clickstream analysis, web and mobile behaviours revealed browsing, purchasing and interaction trends which could be used for personalised and targeted advertising, marketing and other business activities. Meaningful feedback and information collected from interactions could be subsequently analysed through various mining tools. Opinions, sentiments, discussions, feedback offered businesses a two-way conversation with consumers instead of one-way information dissemination. This dialogue between the user and business yielded profitable results and sustained business relationships.

Web 2.0 which is primarily about social interactions on the web can yield invaluable data. WI&A (Web Intelligence and Analytics) gained significance due to advent of Web 2.0. User generated forums, online discussions, blogs, social networking yield unstructured textual or audio-video data to be used for meaningful analytics. Clickstream analysis can be a treasure cove for browsing, usage and eventual purchasing patterns. Web analytics provides useful inputs for website designing, product optimization, customer analysis, market structuring etc.

BI&A 2.0 is all about analysing and deriving profitable insights from unstructured web and mobile content being continuously generated. Resultant trends, patterns and visualizations can form basis of informed decision making and strategizing. Any user interfaces such as websites, company blogs, product optimization etc. can be customised after a careful study of user trails. The Human Computer Interface (HCI) becoming critical in almost all transactions, its design and acceptability become crucial game changers. Content generated by the user such as forum, group chatter and blogs contain opinions and feedback which can be effectively utilised for improvements and enhancements.

The techniques used are sufficiently advanced such as text, web, opinion and sentiment mining, spatial, social and network analysis.

c. BI&A 3.0

Mobile computing devices have outnumbered desktops in 2011 (The Economist). Sensors are recording every movement of things and people. Foot-prints of location, context, motion, touch, audio and video are being generated. Individuals are not just interacting with humans but with inanimate objects such as cars, smart devices etc. to generate massive amounts of data. Sensor based GPS, Internet enabled devices, RFID, bar codes, smart tags etc. are also continuously generating data. "Internet of Things" (IoT) result in location and person specific, real time big data, offering immense challenges as well as opportunities.

Exhibit: Business Intelligence: The Evolution

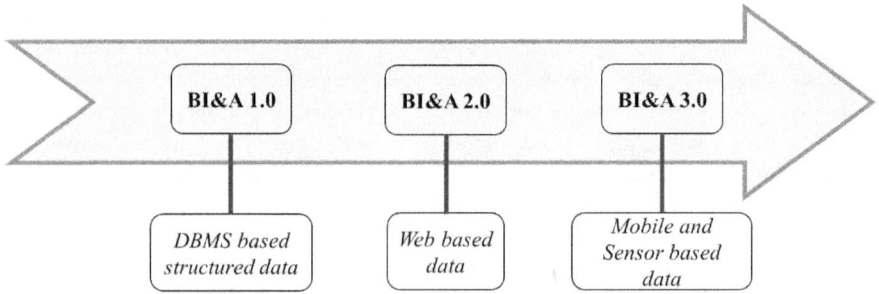

3. BUSINESS INTELLIGENCE & ANALYTICS (BI&A)

Business Intelligence has always been used as an encompassing terminology for all architectures, databases, processes and methodologies, tools and technologies, applications which can be used for collecting, storing, organising, analysing and reporting data. Hence it is also referenced as Business Intelligence and Analytics (BI&A). It has an eclectic combination of data gathering, storage, knowledge management and analytic tools to give internal and external information to decision makers for planning and monitoring purposes. Practitioners make a clear distinction between BI&A software which is usually a standard off-the shelf product, tools or applications which are "add-ons" installed / configured for a specific purpose and a BI&A solution which includes the entire architecture of servers, networks, operating systems etc.

Hence, essentially an array of tools such as databases, data marts, data-warehouses to store data; ETL tools to cleanse and organise data; varied processes such as data and text mining, reporting, and visualizations; and tools such as dashboards, decision support technologies, analytics all come under its broad scope. Information and communication technologies of course form the integral part of the BI framework.

The data accumulated from internal, operational or external stakeholders is collated and fed into Data Warehouses. This data may be of varying formats, quality, granularity and multimedia so the task of integrating, cleaning and loading assumes complexity. The data may be structured or unstructured and may call for use of extracting, processing, indexing etc. Big data emanating from mobile and sensor devices and its resultant collection, storage, analysis and visualization has become an inseparable management task. Repeated i/o operations significantly impact querying time and hence repeated tasks such as summarisation, aggregation, is speeded by materialization of views or caching of results.

Exhibit: BI&A

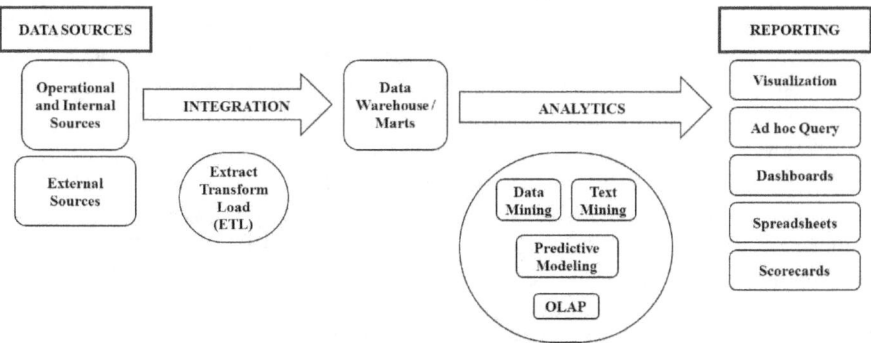

Extracting, Transforming and Loading enterprise wide data into Data Warehouses, and subsequently simple querying, OLAP (Online Analytical

Processing), and resultant visualizations help extensively in decision making. Business Performance Management with the help of tools such as scorecards, dashboards etc. help monitor, analyse and visualize metrics attached to critical processes. Various data mining techniques such as association analysis, segmentation, clustering, classification identify patterns and trends in data – helping to target profitable customers, assist in shop floor placing etc. Anomaly detection identifies outliers or exceptions. It is also a tool for auditing by helping to identify possible frauds. Regression Analysis helps work out causal relationships and thus profitable advantageous relationships may be fostered. Predictive modelling helps plan and strategize proactively.

4. ADOPTION DETERMINANTS

There may be several Technological, Environmental and Organizational (TOE) factors which may accelerate or impede implementation of these technologies. The biggest road-block to any technology could be the initial inertia against change. There may also be lock-in periods of an existing technology both in terms of cost and time. Again, sometimes a technology gets stuck in "expert" phase where it does not trickle down from the experts hired to execute it. The "IT" must also focus more on "I" – the people than "T" – the technology. Hence understanding of behavioural aspects of technology implementation is of equal importance.

There are several theories to substantiate the constant interplay between people and technology. Any innovation goes through adoption and scaling phases. (Digital Infrastructure Theory). After initial phases, as resources are being invested, more and more people start adopting the new technology. This leads to scaling – expansion of reach, both in terms of users and functionalities

Policies and processes of the organization and prevalent culture can also affect the implementation process. Sometimes this onslaught of technologies may result in a gap in acceptance and implementation because of several people related issues such as lack of technology skills, resistance to change and required change management. Compatibility of new software with existing culture, needs, capabilities and infrastructure also acts as catalyst or inhibitors. Sometimes the acceptance and use of the software adds to the social status and image of the worker and hence may act as motivators. Implementation phase must be based on a deep evaluation of user needs and motivations.

Innovative bend of mind and knowledge of IT are the initialising factors for any technological initiative in an organisation. A deep commitment from the top management, organisational readiness in terms of technology, infrastructure and more importantly people, are the deciding factors of successful implementation. The capability of senior members and team leaders to communicate its importance to their team also adds to its acceptability. Further they must establish a clear link and relationship between the organisation vision and mission with the BI&A platform. The Business Intelligence strategy must be in alignment with the overall organisational strategy.

Exhibit: Adoption Determinants

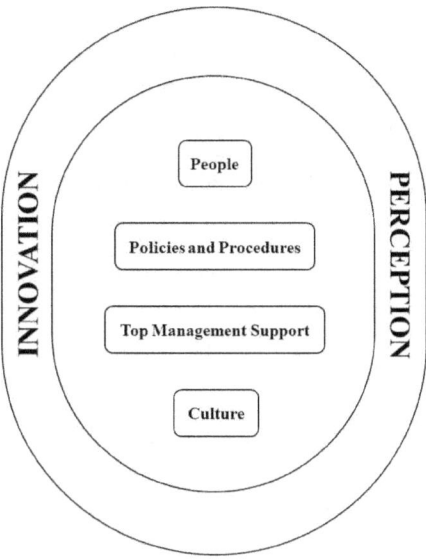

User perceptions and acceptance are inter-related as perceived benefits of implementation act as accelerators. Trialability and result visibility also play vital roles in the acceptance process. Some practitioners have also suggested "relative advantage" as a factor which is defined as how useful a new technology may seem compared to the one already in use. Sometimes the perception of complexity also impedes implementation of technologies. Training can significantly impact user acceptance and confidence levels.

There may also be a very rapid evolution of technologies requiring frequent investments and cost over-runs. Organisation size and scale of implementation may also effect the process of adaption

Privacy and Security are at risk in the process of collecting and analysing people data. There are several ongoing debates about the ownership of personal details of people fed into forms, websites, Government interfaces. Again, copyright infringement of various kinds of content on the web is another area of concern.

5. BI&A FRAMEWORK

SAS, the market leader in business analytics software, has proposed Information Evolution Model (IEM), listing its four dimensions:

a) **Infrastructure:** tools and technologies to collect, store, distribute and apply information.

b) **Knowledge Process:** Role of information in decision making
c) **Human Capital:** capabilities, responsibilities, training, improvement of skill sets of people involved.
d) **Culture:** Social, behavioural and ethical environment. Often the term "soft infrastructure" is used to denote people, procedures, culture, motivation, skills and communication.

The BIA framework consists of 5 major components:

a)   Data Sources
b)   ETL processes
c)   Data Warehouses
d)   Analysis Engine
e)   User Interfaces

Tools of connectivity, transformation, analytics and visualization are also used. Several technologies such as database management systems, data warehouses, ETL, OLAP, BPM are part of the infrastructure.

Steps of the BI & A process are as follows – Data from various data sources such as operational databases, external, databases, customer databases etc. is loaded into the Data Warehouses through the extract-transform-load process (ETL), where the data is extracted from databases, servers etc., cleaned, standardised and then loaded. ETL tools take care of the quality and consistency of data being loaded such as naming inconsistencies, duplications etc. There are associated data quality metrics.

Various specialized analytical tools such as Online Analytic Processing (OLAP), multidimensional analysis, filtering, aggregating, drilling mining, and pivoting of data then can be used. Various types of mining engines such as text, data, sentiment etc. help in in-depth analysis

Then the front-end applications such as reporting servers, dashboards, spreadsheets, visualizations aid decision making capabilities of the user.

A. Big Data

The term Big Data was coined to denote large amounts of data in varied formats. These may be messages, pictures, logs, blogs etc. Big Data is often characterised by the 5Vs – volume, velocity, variety, veracity and value. In most cases such as web, image and sensor data it is unstructured. Quality of input data has a deciding role in the outputs obtained. This data emanating from diverse databases may require extensive integration, cleansing and standardization due to inoperability issues such as inconsistencies in formats, quality, naming patterns etc. Sophisticated tools and techniques are required for analytics of Big Data.

B. DATA WAREHOUSING AND MINING

a) Data Warehouses

These are central repositories where data from all kinds of sources both internal and external are integrated for subsequent analysis and reporting. They are special kind of databases which are subject oriented, integrated, non-volatile, time variant storehouses of data. Data Marts are smaller and more specific to a department/ product/ territory etc.

b) OLAP Servers

These help in analysing data from multi-dimensional perspectives. It has basic operations of consolidation, drilling, and slicing and dicing. These provide functionalities of filtering, aggregating, pivoting, and rolling of data. Various dimensions and/or measures may be the parameters for these operations.

c) Data Mining

This helps in finding hidden trends and patterns of data. Data Mining (DM) also helps in audits as they highlight outliers and anomalies in data sets. There are several tools for DM such as cluster analysis, association analysis, sequential analysis etc. There are several software available for data mining, such as SAS, STATISTICA, Oracle Data Mining (ODM) etc.

C. ANALYTICS

Data Analytics consists mostly of data-mining and statistical analysis to derive useful insights from various kinds of data. Listed below are the major types:

a) **Descriptive:** The data is explored to understand behaviours, demographics, combinations, characteristics etc. This in a way analyses the past.
b) **Predictive:** This is the form of analytics where future trends and behaviours can be predicted by analysing past and present data. Here rigorous statistical techniques are applied on representative samples of data and models worked out, which is then integrated into the population to make accurate predictions.
c) **Prescriptive:** This is sometimes referred to as the "final frontier" of analytics. It goes beyond and combines both descriptive and predictive analytics to find out outcomes of each predicted scenario and then suggest the best option.

Analytics can be for different content types, for different mediums and using different methodologies.

a) Text Analytics

A large part of online content is in textual format – be it emails, survey responses, documents, web pages, social media, blogs etc. Text processing and indexing has been a part of document management systems since long. Information extraction, opinion mining, and entity recognition are some of the commonly used techniques currently. This is done by searching for some words of names, places etc. and classifying them into pre-defined categories. In the same lines, opinion and sentiment mining help in understanding the product / service / organisation feedback over the various social media platforms.

Other applications could be to gauge public reactions to political events/ people, company strategies, marketing endeavours, product response etc.

b) Web Analytics

Having its foundations in statistical analysis and text analytics, web analytics uses websites, web search engines, web log and directory systems for web crawling to help in updating, ranking of websites / pages etc. This helps understand how the users are interacting with the web-pages, what are the user reactions to the landing pages, site layout, complexity etc. Web log analysis helps to monitor usage of web resources. It also helps in social media analytics, analytics of monetization of web resources, evaluating online marketing etc.

c) Network Analytics

This finds its roots in bibliometric analysis to help understand online communities and social interactions. This helps to understand impact, diffusion, network links and relationships. Link Mining helps in understanding or predicting links between a network. This network may be of customers, users, members of a community etc. The links helps understand relationships, usage, collaboration, exchanges and the like. The techniques used may be common-neighbours, graph partitioning algorithms to represent communities as graphs etc.

It finds immense use in identifying terrorist / criminal networks, understanding social or information diffusion, online affiliations, political leanings etc.

d) Mobile Analytics

Mobile computing devices have become ubiquitous and indispensable. They contribute tremendously to the efficiency and effectiveness of the organizational activities. Mobile data generated is detailed, location and context specific and personalised. This acts as a treasure trove for marketers for understanding demographics, behavioural and social patterns. This location and activity specific individualised data can help generate personalised information, advertising and other such inputs to the user. Some notable examples are m-learning, m-health etc.

D. REPORTING

Data collected is analysed through various means. There may be requirements of either routine, periodic reporting or ad-hoc query processing. Data may have dimensions (such as product, customer etc.). These dimensions may be characterised with different attributes for example the customer dimension may have name, age, address etc. Some of these may be associated with measures such as sales, profit, age etc.

Exhibit: Dimensions, Attributes and Measures

There may be three broad categories of users:

a) The first set may use pre-defined reports and metrics.
b) The second set may use these analytics portals to manipulate the reporting parameters and formats within pre-defined boundaries. Another interesting use could be to improve on the already used / defined reports and build / improve on it to deliver better / additional results. There may also be exception reporting functionalities which highlight anomalies of any kind leading to corrective actions and remedial measures.
c) The last set may be data scientists who work with large and unstructured data sets to find out hidden characteristics, trends and patterns of data.

There may also be a spectrum of users as per their trust and usage levels. As coined in a Harvard study – "unquestioning empiricists" trust data over judgement, and "visceral decision makers" rarely do data driven decision making. The ideal variety of users may be "Informed sceptics" who balance judgement and analytics.

As defined by Davis in 2006, there may be again "levels of adoption" which are:

a) **Operate:** Utilisation of BI&A tools for day to day routine working.
b) **Consolidate:** Where data is integrated across various sources for mid-term decision making across departmental levels.
c) **Integrate:** Here data is consolidated in a central repository such as a data warehouse for enterprise wide decision making.
d) **Optimise:** This is when the technology seems to mature and is utilised for deeper analysis in the organisation leading to optimum utilisation of all kinds of resources – people, technology, data etc.
e) **Innovate:** This is the highest level of adoption where the technology becomes an integral part of the organisation and is used to bring paradigm shifts in the functioning of the organisation and bring transformation through innovation.

E. COMPLEX EVENT PROCESSING

These are extremely sophisticated set of tools which help analysing real time / near real-time data – for example to gauge temporal data trends over volatile operational data, stock trading, streaming data, click streams, reactions etc. An essential difference is that it is not first loaded into warehouses for analysis.

6. BI&A IMPLEMENTATION STRATEGY ROADMAP

Implementation of BI&A program needs to follow a very well-defined strategy usually having crucial components:

* BI&A implementation road-map
* Management of all Stakeholders
* Architectural Blueprint
* Upgradation/ Improvement/addition of hardware / software

7. BENEFITS

BI&A provides better quality of information for decision making purposes. "Single version of truth" is by far the biggest gain. An important utility would be in the planning and monitoring of all business processes. These BI technologies help tremendously in increasing the efficiency and effectiveness of any organisation. Business Activity Monitoring (BAM) or Business Process Management (BPM) are important areas where BI&A tools play a vital role. One of the key utility would be to extract desired data subsets from source systems, helping users to view it along diverse dimensions and attributes, drilling or aggregating as needed and often using visualizations to understand / depict results. Scorecards, metrics, visualizations all help in variance analysis and resultant course correction.

Use of various statistical and mining tools help in understanding various trends and relationships between various parameters. These also help the business in understanding its consumer preferences, market scenarios and competitor placing helping it take timely decisions and become an agile organisation. Various analytics methods may also be used to evaluate the accuracy and reliability of self-filled forms. CRM is another key implementation area.

A. APPLICATIONS IN VARIOUS VERTICALS

BI&A has already created its niche in e-commerce, e-governance, marketing etc. It helps to strike a conversation with the stakeholders and "listen" to their needs and concerns.

Steve Jobs had famously remarked that the customers do not know what they want and junked the concept of market research. In present times "big data" can give valuable insights about customer behaviour. When stakeholders are freely voicing their opinion in real-time – Facebook / Twitter etc. there seems to be no need to pay for similar data which may become obsolete by the time it is collated and analysed for use.

a) Marketing

The mobile and web commerce communities are the biggest set of gainers from these set of tools and technologies. By analysing user searches, online behaviours, logs, transactions and user generated content lot of insights could be gained into demographics and behaviour patterns. Resultantly the marketer can consolidate the product positioning by product optimisation and product recommenders.

Some of the techniques used on this unstructured multimedia and social network data could be text and sentiment analysis, association rule mining, database segmentation, clustering and anomaly detection.

A notable example would be the algorithms used by Netflix to analyse user ratings and recommendations. Usage patterns and customer dissatisfaction can be gauged and act as warning signs of customer attrition.

b) E- Governance

Governments across the world are increasingly involving their citizens in various policy and Governance decision making. They are encouraging citizen engagement in all their activities. Citizens are providing valuable suggestions and feedback to various programmes and services.

Even in electoral politics leaders are actively interacting with the citizens for campaigning, voter mobilization, fund raising etc. Citizens can also be observed for their leanings and subsequently influenced and convinced for political affiliations, donations etc.

The tools used mostly are information integration, content analytics, social media and sentiment analysis.

c) Health Industry

Health industry yields another very useful opportunity of using "Intelligence" for patient profiling and eventual care with occasional marketing. Electronic Health Records (EHR), diagnostics, prescriptions, insurance records, medical spends all yield valuable data. The patients' participation in online forums, communities, groups etc. can be factored in their healthcare. This data also helps in analysing patient history, side effects, mental upheaval with the help of sentiment, social, cluster, association analysis etc.

d) Crime Control

With the advent of a plethora of cyber activities, there has been an onslaught of malpractices, fraud and crime. There are several advantages of using "intelligent" agents to counter mala fide intent. Internet chatter, history, server logs are storehouses of data yielding insights into cyber theft, crime and terrorism. Association mining, clustering, spatial analysis and anomaly mapping help in identifying crime prone areas and individuals.

e) Scholarship

The electronic intervention in the education industry has been a disruptive innovation and an immense force multiplier. Institutions have a diverse mix of students. Some learning environments may be limited in faculty and infrastructure. Blended just in time learning and instruction may be a plausible solution. Resultant connectivity gives an enhanced audience. Web enhanced education may incorporate all facets of learning and flip it to ensure a learning experience optimised for time, place and bandwidth. Online pre-reading, coursework and evaluation can map students' learning experience. Personalization of the learning experience and extensive communication with peers and teachers are some of the instant gains. The human brain tends to focus more on spurts of information rather than long drawn ones. Hence feeds, tweets, alerts, updates serve as stimuli more effectively than sustained stream. MOOCs have democratised knowledge

Structured data such as attendance records, grades etc. or unstructured such as feedback, student emails, blogs etc. can all contribute to more informed decisions. Data may be mined from Learning Management Systems (LMS) too. Many useful insights derived such as early signs of student drop-outs, student dissatisfaction may all contribute to effective management.

In constrained learning environments personalized study materials, tips and tricks for easier learning may be a boon for the disadvantaged learners who grapple with disproportionate class sizes and inadequacy of qualified teachers.

The internet penetration level has grown 933.80% from 2000 to 2017 (Internetlivestats). This may present an optimistic picture as shortage of trained faculty, study material and other educational resources can be combated with personalized online learning, video lectures, asynchronous learning systems etc.

8. VENDORS

Each year Gartner releases Magic Quadrants (MQ). MQ uses two-dimensional matrix to show the strengths and differences of technology companies. The importance of graphic tools and visualized data discovery is immense. All big names such as Oracle, Microsoft, IBM, SAS, SAP and even the small players are adjusting themselves to this wave of disruption in analytics.

There are four "mega-vendors" namely Oracle Hyperion, SAP Business-Objects, IBM Cognos, and Microsoft BI.

A. BIG DATA

Big Data requires use of Big data infrastructure such as MapReduce and Hadoop Systems. Hadoop is an open source product from Apache Software Foundation for distributing and managing large amounts of data. It provides a software framework for distributing applications to handle massive amounts of data over clusters of servers. Datameer and Zoomdata are new players in this arena. Introduction of user-friendly front-end tools is deriving more value from these expensive IT acquisitions.

B. DATA WAREHOUSES

Teradata is the market leader in this space and has latest tools and techniques including Hadoop based technologies. By providing functionalities of parallel processing, it allows companies to analyse efficiently. A unique feature available is the option of segregating data into hot and cold depending on how frequently they are accessed.

Oracle has been synonymous with databases since a long time. Oracle 12c Database is a highly optimised and scalable data warehouse product. It has facilities of Flash Storage and Hybrid Columnar Compression (HCC) which enables high levels of compression of data and reduced Input / Output overheads.

Growing popularity of cloud computing has established Amazon as a front-runner with Amazon Web Services (AWS). Redshift, a cloud warehousing solution and associated products have achieved highest customer satisfaction ratings consistently.

c. BI Engines / Suites

- Qlik: It is headquartered in US and provides QlikView and Qliksense, which are BI and visualization solutions. It helps users discover insights and relationships from data. It creates visualizations with the help of simple techniques such as the drag and drop functionality.
- IBM Cognos: IBM acquired Cognos in 2008 and provides BI and Performance Management (PM) products. It has self-servicing tools which helps users to personalise their reports and dashboards.
- Oracle Hyperion: Hyperion was acquired by Oracle in 2007 and has several BI and Business Performance Management (BPM) tools.
- SAS: They are market leaders in statistical and predictive analytics. It has extensive forecasting, text analytics and decision tree functionalities.

d. Visualizations

- Tableau is the undisputed BI market leader with its flexibility and diverse tools.
- Lumira: This a powerful visualization tool from SAP. It can create graphical outputs by integrating inputs from multiple data sources.

e. Open Source

- Pentaho: It is a Business Intelligence software company offering open source solutions for data integration, OLAP, dashboards, mining etc.
- Waikato Environment for Knowledge Analysis (Weka): It is a free software containing visualization tools and algorithms for predictive analytics. Its uniqueness lies in its portability as it is programmed in JAVA. It also supports data mining tasks.

9. CONCLUSION

A famous Harvard study is titled "Good Data does not always guarantee good decisions", yet the importance of Data Driven Decision Making (D3M) cannot be underemphasized. Again, the costs of a technology must justify the investments involved. The value of a decision cannot be less than the costs incurred in the collection of data involved in the decision-making process. There also needs to be some metrices with well-defined outcomes and milestones in place to evaluate the efficacy of BI&A implemented to communicate the Return on Investment (ROI) to all concerned. This will establish their importance even further.

Again, there needs to defined governance structure for the BI&A programme of the organisation. The next wave of BIA of course is in predictive scenarios such as in simulation and extrapolation.

Exhibit: BI&A Framework

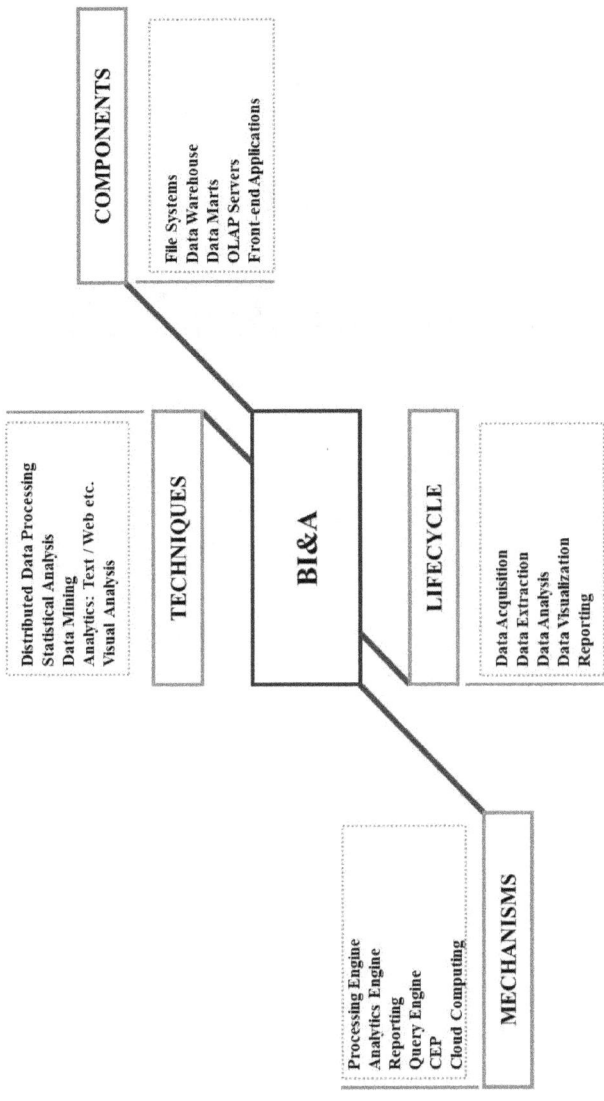

Section

Marketing Analytics

MARKETING ANALYTICS

AUTHOR BIO

Prateek Mangal

Prateek works as the Director – Client Services for SSR Management Consultants Pvt. Ltd. An MBA from Indian Institute of Foreign Trade, Kolkata and International University in Geneva, Switzerland. He is also a Diploma holder in Cyber Law from Asian School of Cyber Laws, Pune. He started his corporate journey with Triton Management Services and served the FMCG giant in Africa and India. He has seven years of experience in FMCG and Manufacturing Industry. Prateek has co-authored and edited a casebook titled "Compendium: Management Cases from Emerging Markets". He has authored several Case Studies and has presented and published research papers on key FMCG and manufacturing issues. He is also a prominent Social Worker and runs an NGO 'Neelabh Foundation' to finance studies of underprivileged children in eastern Uttar Pradesh.

1. INTRODUCTION

Today, marketing function is an inseparable organ of any organization - large or small. Marketing is the most essential pillar of the sales function. The story of onset of marketing departments in companies is very interesting. In the mid 1940's, World War II had wreaked havoc, and there was widespread destruction all across the world. Economic growth of the world was set back by decades. The industries then, were largely manufacturing based and they were the pioneers of post-World War II economic boom. In their efforts to grow, the manufacturing industries soon realized that merely pushing sales was not in tune with customer desires. This realization led to the conception of marketing departments in companies, with the aim to assist the sales function. The companies considered the need for specific initiatives to understand and influence customer psyche to increase their share in the sales pie.

There have been regular breakthroughs in marketing since then, with the positive outcomes from the formation of marketing departments. Around the 1960's, people started becoming brand conscious. People were now influenced by brand images and this recognition led to the formation of marketing companies. Marketing companies were consultants to manufacturing and other industries, providing them with tailor-made solutions. In the 1990's the era of relationship marketing started. The basic idea behind relationship marketing was to focus on customer loyalty and long-term customer engagement rather than short-term goals like individual sales and customer acquisition. The relationship marketing era prevailed for two decades.

With the advent of Internet era in 2000's, there was a paradigm shift. Shops now had online presence to save on infrastructure and operation costs, as well as to reach out to a broader audience. This was accessed using electronic media devices such as desktops and laptops. Customers started giving preference to online shopping with online payment options like debit / credit cards, net banking, digital wallets etc. over traditional marketplace and payment methods.

In the 2010's marketing saw another change in trends with the introduction of social / mobile marketing. This change provided the marketers with a new game changer – Big Data. All the transactions happening online were now being recorded, people made personal accounts for online shopping and furnished details, such as name, age, gender, location etc., which were then recorded and formed a part of Big Data. Big Data provided basis for segregation of customers on different parameters or demographics.

A. CONTEMPORARY MARKETING

Forrester Research coined the term "The Age of the Customer", where customers, and not the companies, are driving business decisions. Trailing on the same lines, contemporary marketing focuses on customer orientation rather than traditional market orientation. It considers approaches like *'co-creation'* i.e. creating a bridge between customer and business to encourage engagement with a product or service and *'shared value'* i.e. considering the market which company is trying to enter, and seeks to offer perks in the said market. Marketers now armed with analytical tools and techniques, along with technological advances like suggestive and predictive engines, are working to better understand customer needs, and offer customization of products / offers as per their liking.

2. BIG DATA

By definition Big Data are extremely large datasets that can be analysed computationally to reveal patterns, trends, and association. In practice, Big Data refers to vast and valuable information collected from customer interactions, social media, along with purchase and browsing history etc. It entails the ever-increasing volume, velocity, variety and veracity of data. Since the advent of Internet of Things (IoT), human beings are producing 2.5 quintillion bytes of data on a daily basis. The objective of storing this huge amount of data is to derive value from it. To derive value from data we need to study it with the help of Big Data skills that include discovering and analyzing patterns, trends and associations that occur in big data.

Any functioning organization generates data. Generally, this data can be categorized under three heads – Customer Data, Operational Data and Financial Data. It is this data which comprises Big Data and is processed for information to benefit the organization.

A. CUSTOMER DATA

Customer data entails data from demographic details to customer surveys, point of sales, online purchases, social media, company loyalty and benefits programs. Customer data can be behavioural, transactional or attitudinal metrics. These data are used to create a more personalized and pleasurable shopping experience for the customer, customized promotions and offers. It can also provide helpful product feedback which is used to improve the products or services.

B. OPERATIONAL DATA

Organizations today have massive IT infrastructures. These IT systems generate enormous amount of data from their day to day running. Key data variables include user response, application performance logs, error messages among others; and these data together form operational data. Operational data can be related to operations, marketing, resource allocation, asset management, budget etc.

C. FINANCIAL DATA

All the data from sales, revenue, profit-loss and other data which give a view of the financial health of the organization are part of financial data. Financial Data is vital in the service industry; especially in banking and financial services. BFSI sector is turning towards "IoT and Streaming" to increase its reach and connectivity. Big Data is being used to integrate historical and real-time financial data; Big Data is also instrumental in improving fraud detection and tracking of financial crimes.

3. WHAT IS MARKETING ANALYTICS?

Marketing analytics is the practice of collecting, managing, measuring and analyzing marketing performance of an organization through certain processes and technologies. The resultant metrics and visualization are used to maximize the effectiveness and optimize return on investment (ROI) of the marketing process. Marketing analytics gathers data from across all business channels and consolidates it into a common marketing view. With increasing choices every day across all categories of products and services, marketing analytics is playing a pivotal role in enabling marketers garner consumer interest and support for their respective products or services.

Marketing organizations today are combining Big Data with integrated marketing management strategy and impacting three key areas – Customer Engagement, Customer Retention and Loyalty, and Marketing Optimization.

A. CUSTOMER ENGAGEMENT

Enhancing customer engagement and rewarding customer loyalty are two of marketing's key goals. Marketing pundits work to achieve these goals by collecting, storing, and analyzing data about individual customers on individual basis. The analysis of these data provides insights about who the target customer is, what they want, when they want it, how much is their average spending etc. These insights are then used to formulate strategies for targeted marketing and loyalty schemes.

B. CUSTOMER RETENTION AND LOYALTY

Surveys show that business owners invest more time, effort, and resources in retaining existing customers than in acquiring new customers. This accentuates the importance of repeat customers for a business. By storing and analyzing individual customer data reports – what they like, what products and offers make the customers make frequent purchase; the resultant information from these data is used to create targeted loyalty schemes and customized offers.

C. MARKETING OPTIMIZATION

Study of data provides insights to which channels are providing highest ROI in terms of marketing spends, so that better optimization of budget can be done. It helps marketers in optimizing marketing effort by increasing rate of customer acquisition, managing purchasing funnels, upselling, and better targeting audience; along with focus on channels with better returns.

4. BIG DATA ANALYTICS

With the explosion in data generation because of internet, IoT, and other electronic media such as mobiles, wearable tech, logs on internet, social media etc. coupled with the use of Big Data tools and techniques; analysts can now analyze data at a far more granular level. This newfound analytical prowess enables personalized recommendations like never before, that too in real time. This makes Big Data really valuable in marketing context.

Giving appropriate information at correct time to the correct person can result in exponential financial gains. The business decision makers, management and different function heads need richer insights that Big Data analysis can provide but so do front line managers, sales staff, tele-calling staff and everyone else who can make an executive decision to make a sale or act on the information.

Big Data analytics should be used to dig deeper for information. It provides the opportunity to process, analyze and re-analyze data for better decision making. Thus, it can help in developing specific strategies and actions to drive growth.

5. HOW BIG DATA ANALYTICS CAN IMPROVE MARKETING

A. GETTING TO KNOW YOUR 'TARGET AUDIENCE'

Big Data can provide insights on- who the customers are, what they want, when they are most likely to need it, how often they make purchase and when they are most likely to respond during the day. Elana Anderson, Vice President of IBM Enterprise Marketing Management said "Among the advantages that big data brings to marketers, perhaps the biggest are the ability get out in front of customers and prospects and to conduct more effective predictive and prescriptive marketing." Big Data Analytics is required to get to a point where a company can address each customer at an individual level; to service the need of the customer even before the customer specifically states the need.

B. IMPROVE 'CUSTOMER RETENTION AND LOYALTY'

Most single-brand or multi-brand retail chains in apparels or FMCG like Big Bazaar, Shopper's Stop, Lifestyle, Pantaloons etc. now have loyalty cards that store the customer data and provide incentives based on the historical purchase made on that card. These companies also use the data to track which incentives or promotions are most likely to bring the customers to the store.

c. Real Time Personalization

By the use of machine learning algorithms on Big Data, customized offers or suggestions can be floated to the customer in real time. Regular customers get better offers and deals than a first-time customer or anyone else just surfing the website to gather knowledge of the ongoing offers and prices but does not make any purchase. It is instrumental in increasing customer retention.

d. Competitor Analysis

There are several new social media monitoring tools available in the market today that track the activity of individuals on social networks. Tools like Keyhole, AgoraPulse, Brandwatch, Buffer, BuzzSumo, Crowdbooster etc. can be used to collect and analyze competitor's activity and their marketing efforts over social media such as Facebook, Twitter, and Instagram. By the use of such tools a company can have a distinct advantage over its competitors.

e. Using Big Data to Gain Competitive Advantage

With the advances in technology and the shrinking size of storage media; it is getting easier to store vast amount of personal data about individual customers, their preferences, habits, buying patterns, previous interactions with the company. These data are then analysed for predictive behaviour and the information received is used to serve the customers and other potential customers in similar demographic category.

f. Use of Analytics for Pricing Advantage

Marketing and pricing go hand in hand. It does not matter how many leads are provided; if the prices are too high and not in accordance with market prices they will act as a deterrent in making the purchase decision. The idea for pricing is that it should be 'reasonable' and 'competitive' but at the same time provide maximum margin of profit. Here real-time personalization plays an important role especially during online shopping. Immediate incentives, discounts or offers pop-up on the customers screen to persuade him/her to make the purchase.

Additionally, as companies can better monitor and optimize their marketing efforts by the use of Big Data, they can better utilize their marketing budget by focusing on areas providing highest ROI.

6. BIG DATA ANALYTICS IN E-COMMERCE

In the entrepreneurial age that we are witnessing today, many businesses are being set up based on online platforms, e-commerce, and similar hybrid models. Venturing into e-commerce is comparatively easier, the overhead costs are minimal, and there is no requirement of a physical showroom at a prime location to display the products. A warehouse with sturdy supply chain management is required. Since most of the transactions are online, e-commerce companies generate a lot of data. These companies then make use of analytics and marketing analytics to stay afloat in the cutthroat competition. Major functions supported by analytics in e-commerce Industry:

A. ONLINE MARKETING ANALYTICS

An e-commerce portal provides the customers with a virtual environment to make a purchase. As the retailers do not have a physical store with inventory where people can walk-in to shop, the online marketing team of e-commerce companies are constantly on the lookout for better advertising prospects with search engine or other websites, which will funnel more customers on their own website.

B. RECOMMENDER SYSTEMS

Recommender systems are engines that serve a blueprint for navigation through the virtual environment for the customer. Recommender engines are one of the major contributions of analytics to technology. These engines or platforms basically work as a filtering system that tries to predict the ratings or preference of a user for a product.

C. PRODUCT SPECIFIC ANALYTICS

Forecast of sales of a product, customer satisfaction rate for a product etc. come under the purview of product specific analytics. Product specific analytics are generally used for a single product or a family of product.

D. USER EXPERIENCE ANALYTICS

Marketing today is all about customer centricity, customer is the king. Mainly because shifting from one retailer to other is as simple as typing a few characters in the browser window and hitting enter! Providing customers with the most optimized and updated virtual environment is an ever-evolving and non-stop process. How product is searched across the portfolio, What will be rank order of results, What alternative products to offer – are all dependent on user experience analytics.

E. MERCHANT ANALYTICS

Most e-commerce portals work as aggregators; they bring several small merchants together and provide them with a platform to showcase their goods. E-commerce portals and merchants have a symbiotic relationship if one grows the other grows automatically. E-commerce portals use analytics to provide localized suggestions to merchants based on the local demands.

7. WHAT DO CUSTOMERS WANT

A. CONJOINT ANALYSIS

There are different driving factors when it comes to consumers product choices. When a marketing analyst has to determine the most liked and most hated attributes of a particular product, such as – *What are the attributes making people choose KitKat above Perk – Brand, Price, Taste or Size?* After showing consumers several similar products (called *product profiles*) and asking the consumers to rank them according to preference, an analyst can do a *Full Profile Conjoint Analysis* to determine relative importance of different attributes. Basically, conjoint analysis enables a marketer to determine the product characteristics that dictate a consumer's product preference. Here the consumer is asked to rank a variety of product profiles.

The product category in discussion is called a *product set*. It is a set of objects from which the consumer has to make a choice. The consumer may choose to select none of the offered objects. Every product is defined by the *level* of several *product attributes*. Attributes are the variables that describe the product. The levels for each attribute are the possible values of the attributes.

Exhibit: Product Attributes and Levels

Product	Attribute 1	Attribute 2	Attribute 3
Cold Drink / Soda	Brand: Sprite or Mountain Dew	Calories: 0 or 200	Price: Low, Medium or High
Cars	Brand: Maruti, Honda, Tata	Price: Low, Medium or High	Fuel Efficiency: 0-10 km/ltr, 10-15 km/ltr
Antacid tablets	Price: Low, Medium or High	Efficacy: Relief in less than 5 min, up to 15 mins	Side effects: % with side effects: none, 5% and 7%

a) Adaptive/ Hybrid Conjoint Analysis

Sawtooth Software in 1985 came up Adaptive/Hybrid Conjoint Analysis for special cases where the product has high number of attributes which make it hard for the consumer to rank the product profiles as the number of product profiles needed to analyze the relative importance of the attributes and the desirability of attribute levels is very large.

It basically is a two-step method; firstly, the consumer is asked to rank the attribute levels from best to worst. Then, the consumer is asked to evaluate the relative desirability of different attribute levels. After the steps 1 and 2, consumer is asked to rate on a scale of 1 to 9 the strength of his/her preference for one product profile over the other.

b) Choice Based Conjoint Analysis

The consumer is shown several product profiles in choices based conjoint analysis and simply asked to select a product profile from the given options; he/she can select to choose none of the options as well. This makes a consumer's task easier but needs much more mathematical calculations than ordinary conjoint analysis.

8. CUSTOMER VALUE ASSESSMENT

Customer Lifetime Value (CLV) is the estimate of the value which the company will derive from their relationship with that customer. Since it is not known how long the relationship will last, it is normally considered over a 12-month period or its multiples. If a company constantly spends more money on acquiring new customers than the customer generates for the company, the company will soon go out of business. As stated by Pareto Principle, 80% of the revenue comes from 20% of the customers, thus it is highly beneficial for the company to recognize those cash cows and focus on them. Hence, it is very important, from a company's perspective to know a customer's lifetime value.

A. HISTORICAL CLV

One of the simplest methods of calculating the CLV is historical CLV, which calculates the customers lifetime value based on the total amount the customer has already spent on the company. It should be noted that historical CLV at times does not take into account the time of association of the customer with the company. Old customers and new customers are all in the same bucket. Historical CLV is based on past data and hence at times can give misleading results.

Exhibit: Transaction Details

Customer Name	Purchase Date	Purchase Amount
Raju	1st March 2017	INR 200
Raju	15th April 2017	INR 300
Shyam	21st January 2017	INR 250
Shyam	14th February 2017	INR 600
Shyam	21st March 2017	INR 400
Shyam	12th April 2017	INR 350

For the first four months of the year, the average monthly revenue from Raju is (200+300) / 2= INR 250 and average monthly revenue from Shyam is (250+600+400+350) / 4= INR 400.

Adding the two (250+400) / 2 gives a monthly average revenue per customer of INR 325. To find 12 month CLV we multiply by 12 resulting in average CLV of INR 3900.

B. PREDICTIVE CLV

Due to the dynamic nature of the markets and ever-changing customer sentiments, relying solely on historical CLV is neither advisable nor feasible. There are certain methods used to predict CLV, such as extrapolation, supervised learning algorithms, and probabilistic modelling.

a) Moving Averages

Simple moving average is a type of extrapolation technique where a customer's future spending potential is predicted by analyzing the past spending over a period of time. Moving average is better than simple average because it takes into account the recent changes in the spending pattern of the customer. However, if the period is longer, the variations are evened out and if the period is very short, there will be very high variations in the actual results vis-a-vis the predicted results.

b) Regression

Simple linear regression or straight-line extrapolation is similar to moving average but it is useful because it does not take into account the seasonality. As it produces a line of best fit, it overall minimizes the difference between the predicted results and actual results.

If the data has a non-linear shape, polynomial regression can be used to fit the data and provide more accurate predictions. Linear regression and polynomial regression are both available in MS Excel.

9. USE OF S-CURVE TO FORECAST SALES OF A NEW PRODUCT

In many industries where product development takes a lot of research and investment, it is imperative to do a sales forecast of future sales of the product being developed so as to get an estimate if the product is worth the resources invested. "Typical" curves have been found to exist for many technologies. One of the most frequently observed curves on the graph of product sales over time is the S-curve. Just like the alphabet, the curve initiates with a slow start, followed by a period of steep growth, and then eventually reaching a plateau which is representative of many technological capabilities and product life cycles.

Sociologist Everett Rogers in his book "Diffusion of Innovations" gave the idea that the percentage of market adopting a product, cumulative sales per capita of a product, and the sales per capita followed an S-curve.

Exhibit: Shape of S-Curve

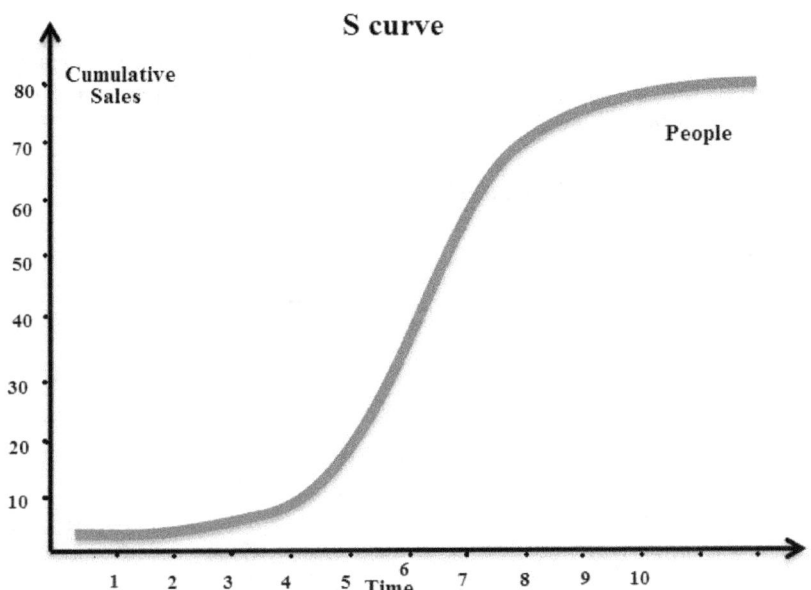

If a few early data points are considered and an S-curve is estimated, following points can be observed:

- **The upper limit of sales:** In the graph above it observed that upper limit is 80.
- **The inflection point:** Inflection point is defined as the time t when the rate at which sales increase begins to decrease. In the above graph inflection point occurs at time 7, where the curve changes from convex to concave.

10. RESOURCE ALLOCATION

It is the job of marketing managers to determine the profit maximizing allocation for products, shelf space and at times the sales force as well. The key here is to understand how the changes in the allocation affect the product sales. To better understand this, the relationship between the resources allocated and the response achieved must be charted out on a graph.

MODELING THE MARKETING RESPONSE TO SALES FORCE EFFORT

A. THE POWER CURVE

$$y = a\,x^b$$

Values of a and b that best fit the power curve can be found with Excel Trend Curve. Assuming $0 < b < 1$, the power curve exhibits diminishing returns i.e. each additional ad yields fewer extra sales.

Exhibit: The Power Curve

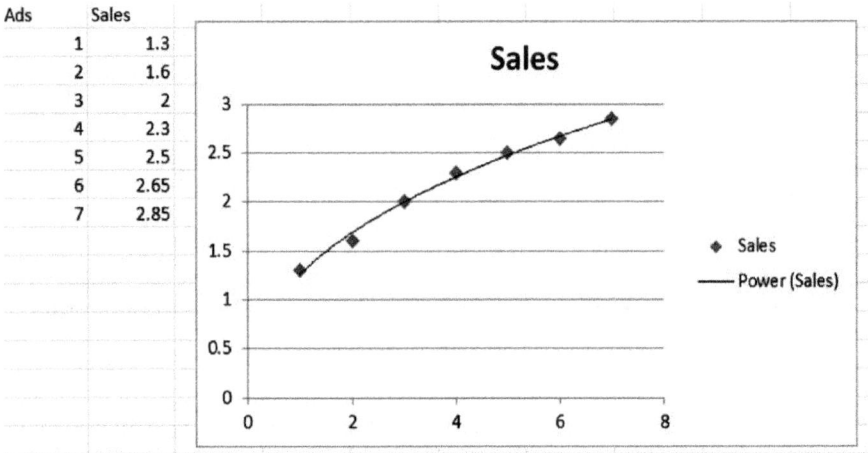

B. THE ADBUDG CURVE

$$Y = a + (b\text{-}a)\,x^c / (d + x^c)$$

The ADBUDG Curve was developed by MIT Professor John Little. This curve is used to chart the graph of response to sales or advertising. The ADBUDG Curve can sometimes be S-shaped, which means that for a small amount of marketing effort little sales response is observed, and for an intermediate amount of marketing effort, increasing returns are observed and finally beyond a certain point, decreasing returns to marketing response are generated.

Exhibit: The ADBUDG Curve

Fitted ADBUDG Curve

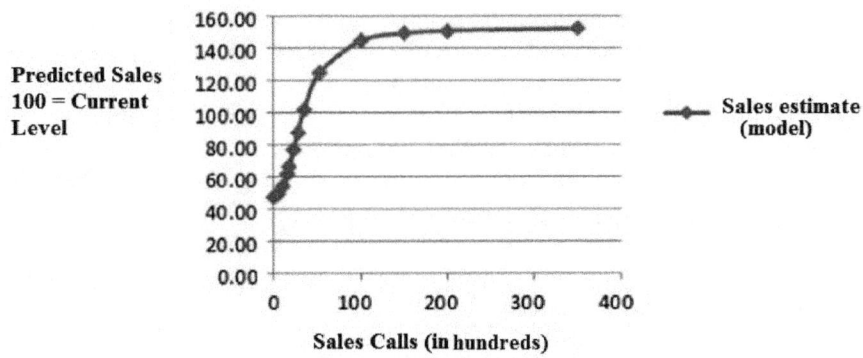

C. THE GOMPERTZ CURVE

y = a * exp (-c exp (-bx))

Any change in profit resulting from allocation of additional shelf space is modelled by the Gompertz Curve. The Gompertz curve is also an S-shaped curve.

11. PAY PER CLICK ANALYSIS

Online adverting in the past years has become a huge business opportunity. In fact, in the second quarter of 2016, Google's advertising business contributed USD 19.1 billion to its parent company Alphabet's total revenue of USD 21.5 billion. Of that USD 19.1 billion revenue, a vast portion is contributed by Pay Per Click (PPC) advertising, where the advertisers pay only when a user clicks through to the advertisers' website. Online advertising is still growing at a rate of approximately 20% per year, so it is important for advertisers to understand how they can enhance their profits by using PPC analysis.

A. DEFINING PPC ADVERTISING

When a customer goes online to purchase a product and searches for the product / information on any search engine like Google or Bing, in addition to showing the search results the search engines also display paid ads relevant to the customers' search. Companies like Google and Microsoft charge advertisers to display their ads when a user does a search for the product or related keyword. It is a very transparent method where the advertisers know that their ad has been viewed or the customer has been redirected to their website.

Before 2002, the prevalent model for online advertising was 'Impressions Model', where the online advertisers paid for *'number of impressions'*, which is number of times their ad was displayed by the search engine. Here it was possible that even after one thousand impressions there was not a single conversion or very few conversions but still the advertiser had to pay for one thousand impressions.

B. PROFITABILITY MODEL FOR PPC ADVERTISING

To calculate periodical profitability of PPC Advertising, the following numbers are needed:

- **Cost Per Click:** The cost that the advertiser has to pay for each click to the search engine company. For calculations let's assume INR 10 per click.
- **Estimated Clicks per Day:** This is the probable number of clicks the advertiser site is expected to have from the ads on the search engine.
- **Conversion Rate:** This is the fraction of clicks on the ads that result in a sale. This is generally based on historical data. Google AdWords average conversion rate across all industries on search network is 2.70%. For calculation let us assume 5% conversion rate.
- **Average Profit per Sale:** This is known to the advertiser or can be calculated from historical data. For calculations let us assume INR 100 average profit per sale.

Exhibit: Profit Calculation

Cost per Click	10
Clicks per Day	25
Conversion Rate	0.05
Profit per Sale	100
Days per Month	30
Conversion per Month	37.5
Profit	3750
Click Costs	7500
Total Monthly Profit	-3750

*Assume 30 days a month.

In the table,

Conversion per Month	= (Clicks per Day) X (Conversion rate) X (Days per Month)
Profit	= (Conversion per Month) X (Profit per Sale)
Click Costs	= (Cost per Click) X (Clicks per Day) X (Days per Month)
Total Monthly Profit	= (Profit) − (Click Costs)

12. SOCIAL NETWORK ANALYSIS

- **Network:** A network is a cluster of nodes connected by links which share resources. In a computer network, computing devices exchange data by the use of a data link. The data link can be a cable link or a wireless link.
- **Nodes:** Individual computing devices on a network are called nodes. When two or more nodes are connected by a link they form a network. Importance of a node can be determined by the traffic it receives. Yahoo, Facebook, Rediff are more important nodes than any personal websites. It is important for marketers to know the nodes that can spread the word for their products, and generate enough traffic to influence customer sentiments.

What was once word of mouth; has now been replaced by social media. People are connected to each other over different social media like Facebook, Instagram, and Twitter among others and share their day to day experiences, recommendations, and opinions over social media for their followers to see. Celebrities have huge online fan-following who watch every update by them very closely. Any update is instantly dispersed to millions of people at a time. Any positive or negative user experience literally travels at the speed of light and possesses the power to make or break brands.

The incredible reach of social networks at the same times provides an opportunity to marketers get a holistic view of the consumers, reach a multitude of customers at minimal costs. Social Network Analytics plays an important role by the means of social listening, context analysis etc. providing insights, such as – What is the brand presence and perception of a particular brand; What should be done to increase the reach and influence the perception in a desired manner. Social Media Monitoring Tools like Hootsuite, Klout, TwentyFeet, PeerIndex etc. help marketers get insights into social media activity of customers.

Klout Score: Klout is a website and mobile app that uses social media analytics to rank its users according to the social influence they have by the means of 'Klout Score'. Klout Score is a numeric value between 1 and 100, it is an indicator of the influence of user's social media activities based on the reach and response of the posts. Ex-President of the United States of America, Barack Obama had a Klout Score of 99 in 2013.

13. VIRAL MARKETING

Viral marketing is a marketing strategy that propagates a marketing message by using websites or social media users to other websites and users, thereby creating a ripple effect and an exponential growth in the reach of the message and it effect and influence.

To make a viral marketing campaign work, one needs to give the right message to the right messengers in the right environment.

- **Messenger:** Market Mavens, Social Hubs and Sales People are three types of messengers that are required for the transformation of an ordinary message to a viral message. *Market Mavens* are information specialists who are on the 'pulse of things'. They are generally the first ones to be exposed to a message and they relay it to their immediate social network. *Social Hubs* are people with remarkably large number of social connections over different social media; they often work as bridge or connectors between sub-cultures. *Salespeople* may be needed to receive the message from Market Mavens and amplify the message by making it more persuasive and relevant, and then pass on the new message to social hubs for further distribution.
- **Message:** For a message to become viral, it should be sufficiently interesting and memorable enough to be sent to other users, to spur a viral marketing phenomenon. The message should be engaging and unique so it has a 'must-see' element or is simply infectious and is propagated widely.
- **Environment:** In addition to the timing and context of the campaign being appropriate, the right environment is also crucial. Minor adjustments to the environment can lead to manifold increase in the results as users are very sensitive to the environment. Based on the context of the message it is propagated on social media like Facebook and Twitter etc. or sent to selected groups on Whatsapp and Viber etc.

14. TEXT MINING ANALYSIS

A large portion of (Big Data) uploaded online on day-to-day basis is unstructured data i.e. movies, clips, blogposts, Facebook posts, tweets etc. To analyze this data and take reliable information out of it without a methodical approach would mean that a person is literally watching every video uploaded and reading every Facebook post to gather the required information. In the heart of all this unstructured data i.e. hundreds of Gigabytes of videos, posts and tweets lies something which is of great importance to a marketer – consumer sentiment.

With the advent of IoT people have become more and more connected; every minor detail of life is now sneaking its way on to the internet. For example, while watching movies people do social media *"Check-in"* into a multiplex on Facebook, with *"hashtags"* #friendsfun #bestplace, later posting the movie review on Facebook, Twitter - #AwesomeMovie #lovedit. Just one status update has review about a place and a movie. The datasets from which text mining can derive meaningful insights are virtually endless.

Text Mining Definitions

A relevant collection of documents is called *Corpus*. To establish the effectiveness of Vodafone Ad with Zoozoo's, all the tweets containing references to Vodafone and Zoozoo's will be the corpus.

A *Document* will be collection of individual words, which are called *Tokens*. For Example, A Facebook update - "Vodafone add zoozoo's are the cutest little things!" consists of eight tokens.

In an update related to advertising, the words 'ad' and 'ads' are treated as the same token and the process of combining related tokens to one token is called *Stemming*.

The common words like 'the', 'and', 'that' etc. are called *stopwords*. These stopwords add to the processing time and do not provide any insight to the text, therefore they are removed. This process is called *stopping*.

When an attempt is made to develop an algorithm to automatically classify the attitude of the text (data) as favorable or unfavorable, it is known as *Sentiment Analysis*.

15. USING MARKETING ANALYTICS TO DRIVE GROWTH

The development of better analytical tools, techniques and approaches in recent times has added a lot of firepower to the armoury of the top management leaders and business decision makers. It is notable that though advances in analytics provide the opportunities to increase growth of the company and Marketing Return on Investment (MROI), organizations are confused with the multitude of choices on offer. This frequently results in over-dependency on just one planning and performance-management approach. The best way for top management to increase the effectiveness of marketing efforts is to integrate Marketing Return on Investment options in a way that it utilizes the best assets of each option. It is estimated that use of integrated analytics approach can save up to twenty percent of spending on marketing.

A. ANCHORING MARKETING ANALYTICS TO STRATEGY

It is an ongoing practice in most of the organizations where the marketing budget is largely allocated on the basis of previous year's budget, or on the business line / product which has performed well in the recent quarters. This is bound to happen till the time there is a strategy anchor in place. These traditional methods basically turn into shouting matches or display of convincing skills, and the budget is allocated to the department that has the strongest presence in the meeting, rather than the products or departments that need to defend their current position in the market.

A better approach is measuring the proposals based on their ROI, economic value, and recovery window. Evaluating options based on fixed meaningful parameters provides a consistent view of all the components, and these results can be viewed under the light of certain pre-existing conditions such as individual threshold for certain media, baseline spending, and any prior commitments.

Identifying the target customer and understanding their buying behaviour is one of the prerequisites in building an effective MROI. With the technological advances in the yesteryears there has been a radical change in the consumer behaviour, old ways of thinking such as the marketing 'funnel' normally do not apply anymore. Consumer behaviour is now subject to many different moments of influence. Consumers do a lot of research about other consumer's 'purchase and aftersales experience before making the smallest of decisions. This results in the buying process becoming much more dynamic and a funnel approach that prioritizes on generating as much brand awareness as possible.

B. MAKING BETTER DECISIONS

Big data has brought a revolution in the marketing analytics world, with more and more data sources to analyze. The science of marketing analysis has found increasing support. Business acumen is required to validate or challenge approaches to study and utilize data. At the same time creativity is also equally important for developing new methods of using data or finding new methods of unlocking data for better insights. Since data availability and quality rules the roost, data 'soft' skills become particularly useful. Any challenges faced will not hinder the use of data for better decision making if the following points are taken into consideration.

C. IDENTIFY THE BEST ANALYTICAL APPROACHES

Today there are a number of options available in the market that can be used to support business strategy as well as to make the right marketing mix. Organizations need to evaluate the pros and cons of each of the tools in contention. For non-direct marketing, there are various choices. Advanced analytics approaches such as Marketing-Mix Modeling uses Big Data to determine the effectiveness of spending by a channel. This approach takes into consideration external variables such as seasonality, promotional activities and competitor activities. This reveals any changes in individuals and segment over time (longitudinal effects), and differences among online, offline and advanced models such as social media activities (interaction effects). Marketing Mix Modeling needs high quality historical data on sales and marketing spending but it can be used for short-term tactical planning and long-term strategic purposes. Also, it cannot measure activities that have minute changes over time. It needs in-depth econometric knowledge to gain perspective into the models and a scenario planning tool to model budget implications.

Factors such as reach, cost, and quality (RCQ) breaks down each touchpoint into its component parts – the exact number of target customers reached, cost per unique touch, the quality of the engagement, using both data and structured judgment. Marketing Mix Modeling is not feasible in cases where data is limited, such as when there is constant spending throughout the year and in cases where the marginal investment affects are harder to isolate. In these cases, such as when media is always-on, RCQ comes into play. It brings all the touchpoints back to same unit of measurement for the sake of equitable comparison.

There are other emerging approaches like Attribution Modeling. As advertising spending is shifting online, attribution is becoming progressively vital for online media buying and marketing execution. Attribution Modeling talks about the set of rules or algorithms that dictate how money for converting incoming traffic to sales is allocated to touchpoints on the internet, such as an online advertisement, e-mail campaign, social-networking feed, or website etc.

D. Integrate Capabilities to Generate Insights:

Companies are run by individuals, who can develop preferences. Hence at times organizations rely on just one analytical method. However, the best returns are harvested from an activity when different MROI tools are used in tandem to reduce any inherent bias of any one technique. This provides the business decision makers with the flexibility to reallocate budget towards high yielding activities.

To put the values of different approaches on common platform for comparison purposes, marketers develop common response curves across different analytical techniques. The company can then use a decision-support tool to assimilate the results, allowing business decision makers to track the marketing performance on a near-real-time basis and also adjust it as and when needed.

While adjusting the mix, it can be tempting to allocate a significant part of the budget to short-term initiatives that yield high Return on Investment. This bias is served by the fact that a lot of data comes from customers engaging in short-term behaviour. This short-term effect typically only consists of 10-20% percent of total sale; while the brand which is a longer-term asset, accounts for the rest. Organizations need to ensure their marketing mix models are capable of scrutinizing marketing efficiency over both time horizons – short term as well as long term.

E. Put the Analytical Approach at the Heart of the Organization

If an organization is not optimally staffed with people well versed with analytics, often an easy way out is to outsource the analysis, or create an internal analytics group and give the job to them. However, when the results submitted by the outsourced entity or internal analytics group are considered, the same decision makers are sceptical about implementation of the results as they do not have faith in the numbers or do not understand them.

To overcome this situation marketing department must work closely with data analysts, data scientists and other marketing researchers to formulate hypotheses, fine tune the results and question any standing assumptions. Companies need to bring on board experts who do both, understand the hypotheses as well as speak the language of business.

Speed and agility of decision making are also important. Insights from the consumer decision analysis and the marketing-mix allocation should be updated to the tactical media mix. Actual results of implementation as they come in should be compared with target figures set during planning, and budget should be adjusted accordingly. Attribution Modeling is especially helpful in cases where there is in-process change in an ongoing campaign, as digital spending can be altered on very short notice.

There is an inherent pressure on business decision makers to demonstrate ROI from a diverse portfolio of marketing initiatives. Due to the advances in Big Data technologies, data to make better decisions are available, and so are the analytical tools.

16. MARKETING ANALYTICS TOOLS SHAPING THE INDUSTRY

Many software development firms are coming up with increasingly better marketing analytics tools. There are various marketing analytics tools available in the market today and there are numerous companies that are making use of these analytical tools in an extremely efficient manner. Some software leading the market are:

A. ADOBE MARKETING CLOUD (AMC)

Adobe Marketing Cloud is an end-to-end digital marketing platform with most complete set of integrated marketing solutions. It is a powerful cloud-based platform for Business to Business (B2B) companies that use the web to find their leads. Adobe Marketing Cloud includes a set of analytics, advertising, social, targeting, media optimization, Web experience management and content management products aimed mainly at the advertising industry that can be utilized very well to track all of a company's analytical needs. AMC is hosted online on Amazon Web Services.

B. GOOGLE ANALYTICS

Google Analytics is a popular analytics tool and a tool of choice for marketer, entrepreneurs and anyone else on a shoestring budget. Google Analytics is a free software and is incredibly feature-rich and rivals many enterprise-level solutions. Since it is free for public use, there are numerous people using it and making tutorials explaining how to use it. This makes it easier for new users to use the tool and find trouble shooting help free of cost.

c. Mixpanel

Mixpanel is a web presence tracking tool and it tracks comprehensive user behaviour to give the marketers a detailed look into how the customers are spending their time online. The data can be analysed as per the company's requirement. Patterns are observed and insights are gained to evaluates which section of the website gets the most hits, which buttons get clicked on the most and so on. The data received is extremely useful for marketers. For example, marketers can use multifactor analysis to compare retention rates for users based on the marketing campaign that "brought them in" and as a result see which marketing campaigns resulted in the most valuable long-term customers.

17. CONCLUSION

Marketing Analytics gathers data from all across marketing channels, sorts and processes the data, and resultant metrics provides a common marketing view. These resultant marketing metrics provide valuable assistance in taking organization forward. A holistic analytical approach will take into account the entire lifecycle – reporting the past, analyzing the present, and predict / influence the future. It allows for better marketing. Marketing analytics can help organizations identify the specific marketing initiatives across different channels that are contributing to the company's bottom line and focus on them, and at the same time support others that are not performing so well.

MARKETING ANALYTICS: CASES

AUTHOR BIO

Kritika Nagdev

Kritika Nagdev is a research scholar at Amity University and an Assistant Professor at Vivekananda Institute of Professional Studies, Delhi. She has got five years of experience in academia and industry. She is deeply enthusiastic about research and analytics. She has organised a sponsored International Conference on the theme of Business Analytics. Her research interest is in the area of Branding, Service Marketing and IT enabled services. Her teaching interest is in the area of marketing, business strategies and policies, Service Marketing, Branding, and Marketing Research.

1. INTRODUCTION

Customers are an invaluable asset of any organisation and the key to achieve their goals. Changing customer behaviour and subsequently reinventing the way products are made and delivered is one of the foremost challenges companies face. The way customers evaluate and purchase products has to be understood by companies. Hence, organizations need data to understand which customers are no more interested in their products or services. What are their buying patterns? What kind of deals are they interested in while buying a product? The answer to these questions can be arrived at by effective deployment of customer analytics by these organizations, which involves the efficient and constructive use of customer data.

Democratization of Internet and advent of social media has led customers to be more informed, instrumented and connected. Customers today do not hesitate to interact with companies and use all the available channels (offline, online, mobile and social). Customers also appreciate personalized experiences.

Organisations utilise large amount of data to describe customers' past buying behaviours, predict future behaviours, and suggest new ways to influence future purchasing decisions. From credit card transactions and online shopping carts, to customer loyalty programs and user-generated ratings/reviews, the data is collected in repositories to extract useful patterns of evolving customer behaviour. As a result, intuition is no longer sufficient to understand the customer. Data driven marketing is based on the customer insights data. Organizations increasingly focus on customer needs and preferences to transform their marketing, communication and sales experiences.

Customer Analytics initiative by Wharton University defines customer analytics as the collection, management, analysis and strategic leverage of a firm's granular data about the behaviour(s) of its customers. It is essential to get individual-level data to forecast, based on observed behavioural patterns. The organisations fetch data not only from one delivery channel but all systems which customers can use. These analyses help companies to construct strategies to acquire new customers, retain the existing customers and optimize strategies to avoid customer churn propensities. Hence, it is contended that customer analytics has created its own distinctive identity in analysis and decision-making theories.

This chapter aims to prepare students and professionals to understand and analyse customer data with the help of customer analytics tools. The readers will gain by learning the concept of Customer Analytics and its most relevant techniques used by companies around the world. The techniques are elaborated and explained by way of sample examples. The readers are expected to have basic knowledge in statistics and holistic marketing to follow this chapter. The chapter will cover the three most relevant techniques:

a) Factor Analysis as an application to understand customer insights, their needs and preferences.
b) Cluster Analysis as a tool for market segmentation.

c)   Multi-Dimensional Scaling (MDS) as a tool for market positioning through reflecting the gap in the current market offerings.

2. FACTOR ANALYSIS

"It is a type of analysis used to determine the underlying dimension of set of data, to determine relationships among variables, and to condense and simplify a data set."

The objective of factor analysis is to summarize a large number of original variables into a small number of synthetic variables, called 'factors'. Determining the factors which are present in the data has several applications in marketing.

- Condensing and simplifying the customer data.
- Testing hypotheses about the structure of a data set.
- Determining the underlying dimensions of the data.
- Identifying market segments and positioning products.
- Developing perceptual maps.

Factor analysis deals with the identification of factors most important to the customers. It can be utilised to examine underlying patterns or relationships for a large number of variables and to determine whether the information can be condensed or summarised in a smaller set of factors or components.

Perceptual maps are drawn with factors as the axes. The original attributes are incorporated into the map as vectors such that direction of line indicates nature of association with the factors and length of line indicates strength of association.

For example: A1, A2, A3, A4, A5, A6 are the attributes which can be condensed into two factors F1 and F2. The relation of this attributes with F1 and F2 has to be calculated by finding out the correlation among each factor. Correlation can range from -1 to +1.

For example, F1 = (A1 (+), A2 (-), A4 (+), A5 (+)); F2 = (A3 (-), A4 (-), A6 (+)), then the perceptual map for F1 and F2 is as follows:

Exhibit: Perceptual Map of F1 and F2

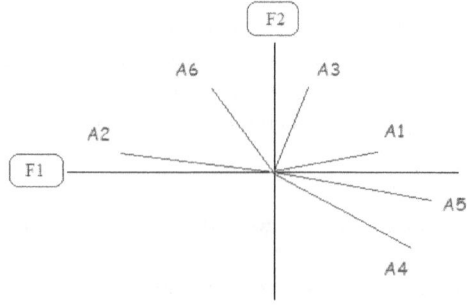

A. Factor Analysis used in Marketing Analytics

To continuously improve the company's offerings, it is important to know the exact reasons customers consider when purchasing a product. Purchasing criteria could vary from a small number (2-3) to large (15-20). It is essential to understand the significant underlying drivers of buying behaviour for a product or service.

Factor analysis helps to reduce the complexity of attributes or features into relevant factors. The analysis establishes correlations between attributes or variables to exact factors. Factors thus created provide insight into relevant psychographics of target customers.

Subjective element in factor analysis will increase or decrease and is controlled by splitting respondents into two groups and extracting factors separately. If the factors are similar, the analysis is reliable.

B. Case: Two-Wheeler

A two-wheeler company desires to understand customer preferences. For this purpose, they initially conducted exploratory research and identified an exhaustive list of variables that could possibly influence buyer behaviour.

These variables were then evaluated for the significance of impact on customer preferences at 90% confidence level. The shortlisted variables were then converted into a questionnaire in the form of statements. Respondents were asked to provide their responses on 5-point likert scale where 1: strongly agree, 5: strongly disagree. An extract of questionnaire as well as the data extract are shown below.

The shortlisted variables are:

1. Use two-wheeler because it is affordable
2. It gives me a sense of freedom to own a two-wheeler.
3. Low maintenance makes it economical in long run.
4. A two-wheeler is meant for men.
5. I feel powerful on my two-wheeler.
6. Some of my friends who do not have a two-wheeler are jealous of me.
7. I feel good when I see ads for my two-wheeler.
8. My two-wheeler gives me a comfortable ride.
9. I think two-wheeler is a safe way to travel.
10. Three people should be legally allowed to travel on a two-wheeler.

The steps involved are:

1. Prepare data and variable view
2. Choose Analyze » Data Reduction » Factor
3. Select Rotation » Varimax

Interpreting the output

To identify the major factors influencing customer preferences

Eigen values are checked in the Total Initial Eigenvalues column in Total Variance Explained table. The number of components with Eigen value greater than one determines number of factors.

To determine the % total variance in the data explained by the abstracted factors cumulatively

In the same table of total variance explained, Percentage (%) variance value is checked. Each respective factor value determines most important factors as per the customers.

For an acceptable factor analysis

a) The Eigen value of factor should be greater than 1.
b) Percentage (%) of total variance explained cumulatively by the factor extracted with Rotated Component Matrix table which are greater than '0.7' and also which are less than '-0.7'. The researcher has to name them according to the variables characteristics, the name should be such that it incorporates all the significant variables.

Exhibit: Rotated Component Matrix

Rotated Component Matrix[a]

	Component		
	1	2	3
afford	.126	.313	.780
freedom	-.181	-.639	-.107
maint	-.116	.604	.594
manveh	.970	-.064	-.006
powerful	.964	.131	.063
jealous	.945	-.140	.030
feelgood	.971	.024	.106
comfort	-.262	.848	.101
safe	.010	.881	-.044
legal	.063	-.149	.874

Extraction Method: Principal Component Analysis
Rotation Method: Varimax with Kaiser Normalization

In this case, as per customers responses, the following factors influence their perception towards a two-wheeler brand:

F1- Man vehicle, Powerful, Friend jealous, and Ads makes feel good can be labelled as MACHO IMAGE

F2- Comfort and Safety could be named as PRODUCT FEATURE

F3- Affordable, Legal could be named as ECONOMY

3. CLUSTER ANALYSIS

"It is a market segmentation technique, used for separating objects into mutually exclusive groups such that the groups are relatively homogeneous."
The concept of market segmentation is based on the principle that the market comprises of heterogenic customer needs (Beane and Ennis, 1987), and therefore different groups of customers exist where individuals in each group are similar in certain ways.

Cluster is group of target customer who are similar in:

a)   Buying behaviour
b)   Demographic
c)   Psychographic

Cluster analysis is done for:

a)   Customer characteristics
b)   Customer response

Cluster analysis is used for market segmentation. The methods for cluster analysis are:

a)   Hierarchical clustering / Linkage method
b)   Non-hierarchical clustering / Nodal method

A. CASE: FMCG COMPANY

An FMCG company desires to understand the segments in its market based on customer lifestyle, attitude and perceptions. To determine this, they have conducted an initial research and identified the variables that have a significant impact on customer preference. The shortlisted variables were then converted into a questionnaire, a sample of which is provided below for reference. Respondent were asked to provide the responses on 5-point Likert scale where 1 stood for Strongly Agree and 5 stood for Strongly Disagree.

Life style/attitude/ perception segmentation statements (questionnaire)

1. I prefer email to post
2. I feel that quality comes at a price.
3. I think twice before I buy anything.
4. Television is a major source of entertainment.
5. A car is necessarily not a luxury.
6. I prefer fast food and ready to eat food.
7. People are more health conscious today.
8. Entry of foreign companies has increased the efficiency of Indian companies.
9. Women are the active participants in purchase decisions.
10. I believe politicians can play a positive role.
11. If I get a chance I would like to settle abroad.
12. I always buy branded products.
13. I frequently go out on weekends.
14. I prefer to buy on credit rather than buy in cash.

The steps involved are:

1. Prepare data and variable view
2. Choose Analyze » Classify » Hierarchical Cluster
3. Select Statistics » Agglomeration schedule
4. Select Statistics » Cluster Membership » None
5. Select Plots » Dendrogram
6. Select Plots » None
7. Select Analyze » Classify » K-Means Cluster
8. Define Number of Clusters as 4
9. Select Iterate and classify
10. Select Options
11. Select all options in Statistics
12. Select Missing Values » Exclude cases listwise

Interpreting the output

To identify the number of segments from data provided

Number of segment are found out by manual method from the Agglomeration Schedule table.

Exhibit: Agglomeration Schedule

Agglomeration Schedule

Stage	Cluster combined		Coefficients	Stage Cluster First Appears		Next Stage
	Cluster 1	Cluster 2		Cluster 1	Cluster 2	
1	4	5	14.000	0	0	4
2	19	20	15.000	0	0	8
3	2	6	17.000	0	0	6
4	3	4	20.000	0	1	12
5	13	16	25.000	0	0	9
6	2	18	26.000	3	0	14
7	1	14	28.000	0	0	10
8	11	19	29.500	0	2	11
9	8	13	29.500	0	5	16
10	1	15	35.000	7	0	19
11	10	11	37.333	0	8	17
12	3	12	37.667	4	0	14
13	7	17	38.000	0	0	17
14	2	3	39.083	6	12	15
15	2	9	42.000	14	0	16
16	2	8	45.833	15	9	18
17	7	10	51.000	13	11	18
18	2	7	53.185	16	17	19
19	1	2	56.804	10	18	0

To find out the number of segments columns 2 and 3 have to be referred. One by one all stages need to be observed. Considering stage 1 to 5, which consists of group of respondents numbered (4, 5), (19, 20), (2, 6), (3, 4), (13, 16).

Till stage 5, no numeric is repeated but stage 6 has member (2, 18) but (2, 6) is already existing in stage 3. So, the next step is to group them, i.e., (2, 6, 18)

Likewise, we find cluster (4,5,3,12,2,6,18,13,16,9). (19,20,11,10). (1,14,15). (7,17). So, there are "4" cluster.

Further referring to Dendrogram (by placing any dialog box on the last vertical line), it replicates and confirms the same number of clusters - 4 clusters.

Exhibit: Rescaled Distance Cluster Combine

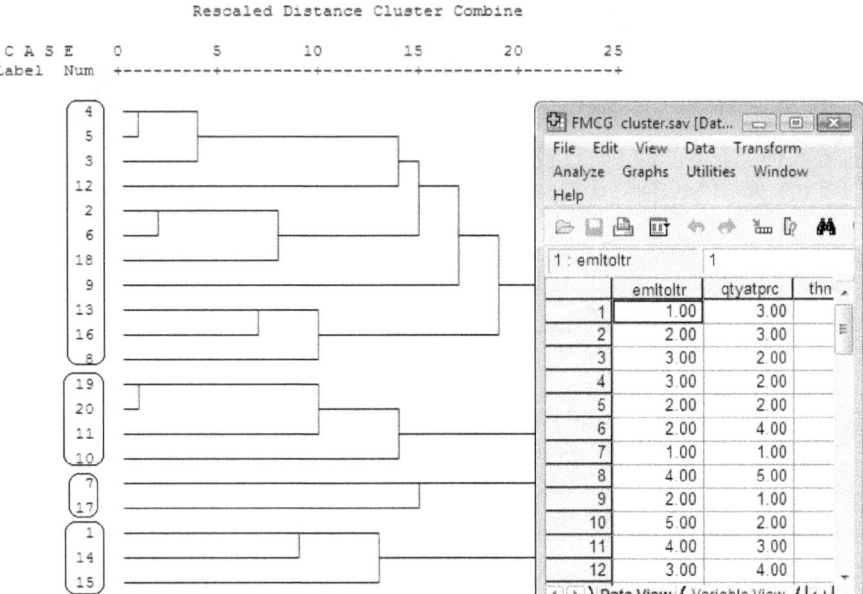

TO DETERMINE WHICH RESPONDENT BELONGS TO WHICH CLUSTER (SEGMENT)

Cluster membership table is the table which confirms the members of clusters. It is the next step after determining the number of clusters by agglomeration schedule. Cluster membership table segregates each respondent/ case into the clusters determined. Hence, agglomeration schedule and dendrogram suggests number of clusters present and the classification of customer dataset is determined by cluster membership table.

Exhibit: Cluster Membership Table

Cluster Membership		
Case Number	Cluster	Distance
1	1	3.143
2	1	2.735
3	4	2.61
4	4	2.969
5	4	2.883
6	2	3.274
7	3	4.724
8	2	3.659
9	1	4.656
10	3	4.441
11	3	3.784
12	4	4.22
13	2	3.064
14	1	3.779
15	1	4.276
16	2	4.552
17	2	4.905
18	2	5.233
19	3	2.706
20	3	3.274

Cluster Membership		
Cluster No.	No. of members	Respondent No.
C1	5	1,2,9,14,15
C2	6	6,8,13,16,17,18
C3	5	7,10,11,19,20

To determine the variable that distinguishes between clusters at 90% Confidence level (C.L).

In the ANOVA table, the member whose value less than 0.1 are the distinguishing variable at 90% C.L. These variables are significant in defining the major characteristics of each cluster.

The profile of each cluster is based on their dominant distinguishing characteristics.

In Final Cluster Centres table, we see only those variables which are distinguishing variables. Each cluster centre value determine the characteristics. It is based on the extent of proximity towards the highest and lowest values of the range. This range has to be determined by the following calculation.

Exhibit: Final Cluster Centers

Final Cluster Centers				
	Cluster			
	1	2	3	4
email_vs_post	1.60	3.50	2.80	2.75
Qual_at_price	2.40	3.33	2.20	2.50
thinktwice	3.60	2.17	3.20	3.75
tv_enterm	3.00	3.33	2.60	3.00
car_necty	3.60	3.83	2.60	2.50
foodpref	4.40	3.50	3.40	4.00
hlthcons	2.20	4.00	1.40	3.50
foreign_ind_co	2.40	1.83	4.60	2.75
womanactv	3.20	2.00	1.80	4.50
politics	2.80	4.00	3.00	3.25
njymovie	3.00	3.50	4.20	4.00
sttl_abrd	1.60	3.17	3.60	4.00
branded_pdts	2.00	3.83	2.40	4.00
goout	2.00	3.83	2.40	4.00
credit_cash	4.20	2.50	1.80	3.75

Considering the first variable email over letter as an example:

Step 1: Plot these 4 points in 5 Point Likert Scale.

Step 2: Identify the Least value = 1.6 and Highest Value = 3.5 for the variable.

Step 3: Calculate the Difference i.e. (3.5 − 1.6) = 1.9

Step 4: Divide it by 4 i.e. 1.9/4 = 0.475

We divide it by 4 because 5 point Likert Scale contains 4 intervals in between.

Step 5: Add 0.475 to 1.6 till we get the highest value 3.5.

1.6 + 0.475 = 2.075, 2.075 + 0.475 = 2.5, 2.5 + 0.475 = 3.025, 3.5 + 0.475 = 3.5

Step 6: Locate the cluster centre points on this scale of 1.6 to 3.5

Exhibit: Final Cluster Centers

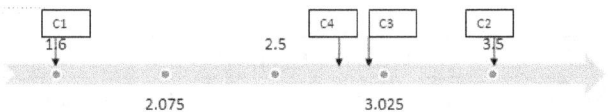

From this scale, clusters' characteristics are concluded as follows:

Exhibit: Cluster Characteristics

C1	C2
Highly prefer email over post	Highly prefer post over email
People are health conscious	People are not health conscious
Agree that foreign company increases the efficiency of Indian company	Foreign company highly influences the efficiency of Indian company
Women may or may not take active part in purchase decisions	Agree that women take part in active shopping
Highly prefer to settle abroad	Prefer to stay in home country
Wearing branded product always	Does not prefer branded product
Always go out in weekends	Not go out in weekends
Strongly avoid purchase on credit	Buy on credit
C3	**C4**
Moderately prefer email over post	Moderately prefer post over email
People are strongly health conscious	People are not health conscious
Foreign company does not increase the efficiency of Indian company	Increase efficiency of Indian company
Strongly agree that women take active part in shopping	Believe that woman does not take active part in shopping
Prefer to live in home country over abroad	Want to live in home country always
Prefer branded product over unbranded	Never wear branded product
Go out in weekend	Stay at home in weekend
Strongly prefer to buy on credit	Prefer to buy in cash

Finally, labels are clustered based on their suitable profiling:

- C1: Modern
- C2: Believers

- C3: Nationalistic
- C4: Strivers

Tables to Remember	
Things to find out	**SPSS Output Table**
No. of segment	Agglomeration Schedule
Respondent Belongs	Cluster membership
Variable that distinguish	ANOVA
Dominant distinguish characteristics	Final Cluster Center

4. MULTI-DIMENSIONAL SCALING

Understanding the raw perception of customer without any aid or stating any attribute is called multi-dimensional scaling.

For example, the company needs to identify why a customer prefers a specific cold drink over others. They shortlist some attributes, based upon which a researcher devises a questionnaire covering the suggested attributes of shape of bottle, colour, sweetness, advertisement, etc. When the researcher interviews a respondent, the responses might be received out of compulsion since it is a forced response. But in reality, the respondent might not consider even one of attributes while having a basic commodity like cold drink.

So, it is argued that these attributes create biasness within respondents. To solve this issue of induced response, Multi-Dimensional Scaling (MDS) is used. MDS is primarily used to create a perceptual map of products. In simple words, brand positioning for a particular group of products or brands as per the customers. It is applicable for positioning of competing brands in a product category.

Raw perception is the customer perception which not influenced by any attribute. It is based on their knowledge, experience and value they derive from the product or brand. It helps to identify the unknown attribute of a product derived from customers' perspective.

Perceptual map is a diagrammatic representation used by companies that attempts to visually present such raw perceptions which might have multiple dimensions. It also helps in positioning the companies' product or brand relative to its competitors.

Hence, MDS captures complex interaction between attributes and brands, as well as determines the dimensions and position of a brand in the mind of customers.

There are two methods which are simultaneously used in MDS:

a)   Attribute based.
b)   Non-attribute based.

The non-attribute based procedure is based on similarity or preference. It is also called the similarity - dissimilarity approach.

In similarity and dissimilarity approach:

a) Conceptual distance measure is used between brands being rated.
b) Distance measure could also be a ranking of distances between specific brand and other brands.

Example: Studying customer perceptions towards soap brands.

Respondent are shown cards with name of two brands on each card. The names on each card are varied.

For example: for studying customer perceptions towards soap brands. Respondents are shown cards with name of two brands on each card. The name on each card varies.

Exhibit: Cards Showcasing Soap Brand Names

All pairs of brands studied are shown. Respondents have to decide brand proximity or differences. Respondent are asked to convey their preferences or difference between brands in terms of their perceptual distances numerically. Scales may be 0-10, 0-20, 0-25, 0-100 etc.

These distances are averaged out across respondents and then converted into a matrix.

Then, the second method of MDS procedure is run to determine:

a) Number of dimensions used by respondent to differentiate the brands.
b) Scores are stimulus on each dimension / stimulus coordinates. The derived scores are interpreted by mapping the output of Direct Response Attribute Scale (DRAS) research on to the dimensions of MDS research.

The following case explains the following.

A. CASE: TELEVISION COMPANY

A television producer desires to understand the brand positioning of eight television brands as per customer perception. For this purpose, they have identified the following brands: Aiwa, Videocon, LG, Samsung, Sony, Onida, Thomson and BPL.

They have conducted a research in two parts. In Part A, an MDS Questionnaire was shown to respondents. Respondent were asked to indicate on a scale of 0-10 the conceptual distances between each brand pair as per their perception. The data obtained was then averaged out across respondents and then converted into misfit. The data is given below for further analysis.

In Part B a match sample was shown as DRAS based questionnaire on a set of attributes. Respondents were asked to evaluate the same eight brands on a 7-point semantic differential scale. A summary of this data is provided below.

Exhibit: Summary of DRAS Table

DRAS Table							
Attribute	**Low**		**High**				**High**
Picture Quality	-	Samsung	BPL	Thomson and LG	Videocon	Sony and Aiwa	Onida
Sound Quality	-	Samsung and Thomson	LG	Videocon	Sony and Onida	Aiwa	
Price (switched)	Thomson and BPL	-	LG and Samsung	Videocon	Sony and Onida	-	Aiwa and Onida
After sale service	LG	Sony	Samsung	BPL	Onida and Aiwa	-	Videocon & Thomson
Brand image	Samsung	Onida and Thomson	Sony	Aiwa	LG	Videocon	BPL

1. Prepare data and variable view
2. Choose Analyze » Scale » Multidimensional Scaling
3. Select Model » Interval
4. Select Scaling Model » Euclidean distance
5. Select Options » Group Plots

INTERPRETING THE OUTPUT

Acceptable condition for determining the number of dimensions that a respondent considers while evaluating the eight brands are

a)   Kruskal Stress < 0.15

b) $R^2 > 0.70$

In our case 3 dimensions are used by respondents.

Exhibit: Dimension Used by Respondents

Iteration history for 3-dimensional solution (in squared distances)		
Young's S—stress formula 1 is used		
Iteration	S—stress	Improvement
1	0.18631	
2	0.15569	0.03063
3	0.15392	0.00176
4	0.15393	-0.00001
Iterations stopped because		
S—stress improvement is less than .001000		
Stress and squared correlation (RSQ) in distances		
RSQ values are the proportion of variance of the scaled data (disparities) in the partition (row, matrix, or entire data) which is accounted for by their corresponding distances. Stress values are Kruskal' s stress formula 1.		
For matrix		
Stress = .09055 RSQ = .86113		

Interpreting the dimensions by mapping the data summary of the DRAS on to the dimension obtained from MDS research.

Exhibit: Interpreting the Dimensions

Configuration derived in 3 dimensions				
Stimulus coordinates				
		Dimension		
		1	2	3
Stimulus Number	Stimulus Name			
1	aiwa	1.9545	.2962	.3460
2	videocon	.0613	1.1370	.9848
3	lg	-.6209	-1.2429	.3121
4	ss	-.9220	-.4411	-1.6871
5	sony	.9783	-1.0898	-.2014
6	onida	.8920	.4307	-.8363
7	thomson	-1.0686	1.6324	-.2905
8	bpl	-1.2747	-.7225	1.3724

Referring to the stimulate coordinates table to evaluate each dimension take dimension one by one. Considering dimension 3 first, and comparing it with DRAS table. Following steps are executed:

1. Identify the highest value in dimension 3 i.e. 1.3724 – BPL. Simultaneously refer to DRAS (direct response attribute scale) table, where attribute BPL has the highest value i.e. Brand image.

2. Identify the lowest value in dimension 3 i.e. -1.6871 – Samsung.

Now, if Brand image contains Samsung as lowest value then there is a possibility that Dimension 3 = Brand image.

3. Lastly it is confirmed by checking the second highest value in this table. If this equals to

DRAS then it sure that

Dimension 3 = Brand image

It may be noted that a dimension contains more than 1 attribute and it may not match with DRAS table as it exactly matching here. We need to take some Flexibility here.

Label each dimension based on their dominant characteristics.

Exhibit: Dimension Labels

Dimension No.	Attribute contains	Name
1	Sound quality + Price + Picture quality	Value for money
2	After sale service	After sale service

If one dimension contains more than one attribute then we have to Label the dimension by keeping all attribute in mind.

The last procedure to follow is creating perceptual map with the dimension plotted as the axis. The position of the brand on this map is based on their stimulus coordinate scope on each dimension.

TO PREPARE THREE GRAPHS BETWEEN ALL THE THREE DIMENSIONS IDENTIFIED.

a) Value for money and after sale service

Exhibit: Value for Money and After Sale Service

Brand name	Value for money	After sale service
AIWA	1.9545	0.2962
VIDEOCON	0.0613	1.137
LG	-0.6209	-1.2429
SS	-0.9221	-0.4411
SONY	0.9783	-1.0898
ONIDA	0.892	0.4307
THOMSON	-1.0686	1.6324
BPL	-1.2746	-0.7225

Exhibit: Brand posit

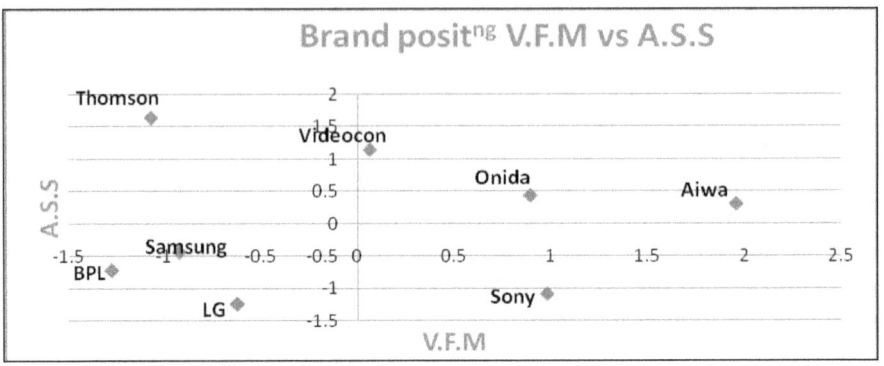

b)   After sale service and Brand image

Exhibit: After Sale Service and Brand Image

Brand name	After sale service	Brand image
AIWA	0.2962	0.3459
VIDEOCON	1.137	0.9848
LG	-1.2429	0.3122
SS	-0.4411	-1.6871
SONY	-1.0898	-0.2014
ONIDA	0.4307	-0.8364
THOMSON	1.6324	-0.2905
BPL	-0.7225	1.3724

Exhibit: Brand posit

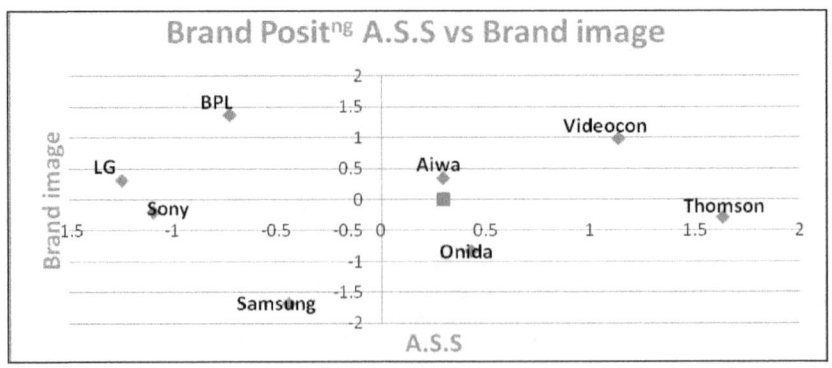

c)   Brand image and Value for money

Exhibit: Brand Image and Value for Money

Brand name	Brand image	Value for money
AIWA	0.3459	1.9545
VIDEOCON	0.9848	0.0613
LG	0.3122	-0.6209
SS	-1.6871	-0.9221
SONY	-0.2014	0.9783
ONIDA	-0.8364	0.892
THOMSON	-0.2905	-1.0686
BPL	1.3724	-1.2746

Exhibit: Brand posit

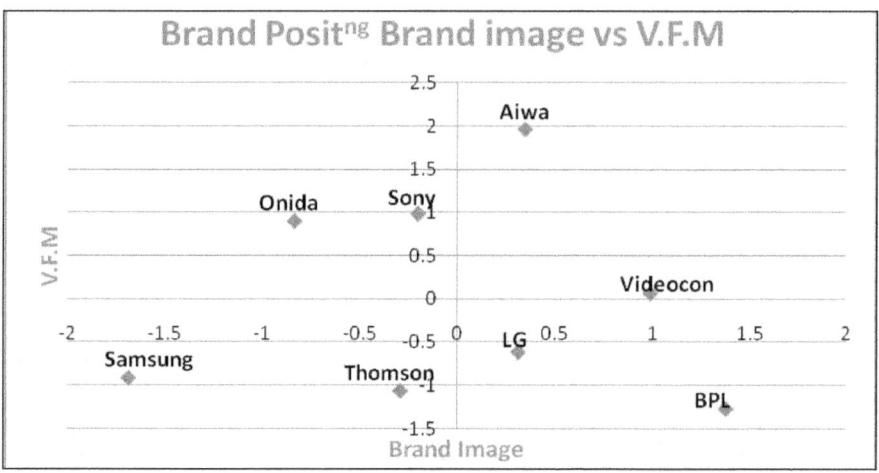

These graphs are prepared by using this table as x and y axis representation and drawing a scatter plot. The points located on the graph represent the position of respective brands.

5. CONCLUSION

As businesses expand into new marketing categories, new technologies are needed to support them. It is important that deployment of these new technologies is in sync. Marketers need to make sure that decisions are taken based on the entire marketing picture, and not merely based on data from individual channels. Marketing analytics considers marketing efforts over a span of time, and is therefore essential for decision making and execution.

6. APPENDIX

Factor Analysis Data Set

Respondent no./Variable names	V1 Affordable	V2 Sense of Freedom	V3 Maint. Cost	V4 Man's Vehicle	V5 Powerful	V6 Friends Jealous	V7 Ads Feel Good	V8 Comfortable	V9 Safety	V10 Legal 3
1	1	4	1	6	5	6	5	2	3	2
2	2	3	2	4	3	3	3	5	5	2
3	2	2	2	1	2	1	1	7	6	2
4	5	1	4	2	2	2	2	3	2	3
5	1	2	2	5	4	4	4	1	1	2
6	3	2	3	3	3	3	3	6	5	3
7	2	2	5	1	2	1	2	4	4	5
8	4	4	3	4	4	5	3	2	3	3
9	2	3	2	6	5	6	5	1	4	1
10	1	4	2	2	1	2	1	4	4	1
11	1	5	1	3	2	3	2	2	2	1
12	1	6	1	1	1	1	1	1	2	2
13	3	1	4	4	4	3	3	6	5	3
14	2	2	2	2	2	2	2	1	3	2
15	2	5	1	3	2	3	2	2	1	6
16	5	6	3	2	1	3	2	5	5	4
17	1	4	2	2	1	2	1	1	1	3
18	2	3	1	1	2	2	2	3	2	2
19	3	3	2	3	4	3	4	3	3	3
20	4	3	2	7	6	6	6	2	3	6

(Variables under Study — Customer Responses)

Responses have been coded as following in the dataset
1 = Strongly agree; 2 = Agree; 3 = Neither Agree nor Disagree; 4 = Disagree; 5 = Strongly Disagree

Cluster Analysis Data Set

Respondent no./ Variable names	V1 email_vs_post	V2 Qual_at_price	V3 thinktwice	V4 tv_enterm	V5 car_necty	V6 foodpref	V7 hlthcons	V8 foreign_ind_co	V9 womanactv	V10 politics	V11 njymovie	V12 sttl_abrd	V13 branded_pdts	V14 goout	V15 credit_cash
1	1	3	5	4	3	5	3	2	3	2	4	1	1	1	5
2	2	3	2	3	4	4	3	2	2	2	4	2	2	2	4
3	3	2	3	4	3	5	3	3	4	2	4	3	4	4	3
4	3	2	4	2	2	4	3	4	5	4	5	4	5	5	5
5	2	2	4	2	2	5	3	3	4	4	5	5	3	3	4
6	2	4	3	3	5	4	4	2	3	4	5	4	3	3	3
7	1	1	2	4	4	1	2	4	2	5	4	3	3	3	1
8	4	5	1	4	5	4	5	1	1	5	3	3	5	5	2
9	2	1	5	3	4	4	2	1	2	1	2	2	4	4	3
10	5	2	4	3	2	5	1	5	3	2	5	1	2	2	1
11	4	3	3	2	1	2	1	5	2	2	4	5	1	1	2
12	3	4	4	4	3	2	5	1	5	3	2	4	4	4	3
13	4	3	2	2	3	3	4	2	2	3	4	3	5	5	4
14	1	2	2	4	2	5	1	3	5	4	3	2	2	2	5
15	2	3	4	1	5	4	2	4	4	5	2	1	1	1	4
16	3	2	1	3	4	3	2	3	2	5	1	2	5	5	3
17	5	1	1	5	1	2	4	2	2	4	4	3	3	3	2
18	3	5	5	3	5	5	5	1	2	3	4	4	2	2	1
19	3	2	4	2	4	4	1	4	1	3	4	5	3	3	2
20	1	3	3	2	2	5	2	5	1	3	4	4	3	3	3

Customer Responses- also termed as cases

Clustering Variables under Study

Multi-Dimensional Scaling Data Set

	Aiwa	Videocon	LG	Samsung	Sony	Onida	Thomson	BPL
1	0.00	3.00	6.00	8.00	1.00	2.00	7.00	8.00
2	3.00	0.00	4.00	6.00	4.00	5.00	2.00	5.00
3	6.00	4.00	0.00	3.00	2.00	4.00	6.00	1.00
4	8.00	6.00	3.00	0.00	3.00	5.00	4.00	7.00
5	1.00	4.00	2.00	3.00	0.00	2.00	8.00	5.00
6	2.00	5.00	4.00	5.00	2.00	0.00	3.00	6.00
7	7.00	2.00	6.00	4.00	8.00	3.00	0.00	5.00
8	8.00	5.00	1.00	7.00	5.00	6.00	5.00	0.00

Section

Financial Analytics

FINANCIAL ANALYTICS

AUTHOR BIO

Vatsal Sahani

Vatsal Sahani is currently pursuing his education from Mayo College, Ajmer (India) where he has secured a perfect 10 CGPA and was awarded a Special Medal for Excellence in Academics along with the Mayo College General Council Scholarship and Mahindra Search for Talent Scholarship for topping the batch. He has cleared the Advance Placements Exams (AP) with Honors and secured a 35 on the standardised ACT test placing him in the 99th percentile globally. Vatsal holds a B1 DELF certification from the Ministry of France where he cleared all the levels with high distinction.

He has represented Mayo at the World School Debates, Slovenia and has been an ambassador to Mayo both in India and abroad through his experiences at the Round Square International Conference in Singapore, and for football in World Sports Festival in Austria and the French Festival in Pakistan.

He is a certified Google Adword, Google Search, Google Analytics specialist and Microsoft Office Specialist (MOS) master who codes in C and C++. Additionally he is a certified Stock Market/MCX Research and Technical Analyst, and has work experience in the financial sector through his internship at Market Hub Stock Broking and in analytics at VRentin Tech Pvt. Ltd.

In 2017, he completed a project with the Harvard University South Asia Institute with recommendation and was accepted into the Young Leaders for Active Citizenship (YLAC) cohort.

In today's highly competitive business environment, organizations have increased their dependence on technology in all facets, including finance. Over the past few years, the role of finance has evolved from basic book keeping and simple financial transactions to a more complex role. The evolving form of businesses today have led to finance impacting the other segments of a business more than ever before. This has pushed organizations to leverage technology in finance. Companies have started to realize that it is just not essential to execute large amounts of work but work in the right direction that provides their firm with the best revenue.

External factors such as economic uncertainty, fluctuating regulations and constantly developing style of business compels leadership in organizations to integrate finance with technology and be more analytical in their approach. Those factors along with the advancement in technologies have led to the emergence of financial analytics which is projected to grow exponentially in the upcoming 3-5 years.

Financial analytics is the art of putting together data in a derivative and comprehensible view from a large set of financial data to aid in decision making. A complex presentation of statistics on a report is not that helpful for a firm until some insight can be derived from it. Moreover, it revolves around reducing risk and leveraging analytics derived from historical data which is not only an efficient but a risk aversion technique as well.

Modernizing one's financial process and information standards reforms the operations of a business organization from inefficiencies and points them towards value added business partnering. Advanced analysis through the integration of finance supported data sources into an organization's core financial analytics system improves fore-sighting and accuracy in businesses. Modelling the finance segment of a business in this manner helps avoid unexpected situations that the business can face in the future. This reduces uncertainty by giving a clear picture and deeper insight into basic metrics with huge impacts on revenue, cost, profitability etc. It helps firms assess their internal strengths or shortcomings and allocate resources accordingly.

Some of the key financial areas include: forecasting, cost management, business risk management, liquidity management etc. There is a constant directive today to leverage better results with less resources which has been a paradigm shift from the past where only repetitive tasks such as collecting financial information with no additions in value added nuances for the organization was done each financial year. Some of the major advantages of financial analytics:

a) **Seek out future trends:** Helps derive useful strategic insights that help companies in decision making and deriving competitive advantage by understanding their core operations and financial activity with greater accuracy.

b) **Comprehend data:** Large organizations often have complex sets of data that can be very crucial for increasing efficiency in their operations but are usually incomprehensible in their raw form. Analytics can help synthesize and bring out relevant results that can be in the best interest of the firm.

c)   **Data Driven Decisions:** Financial analytics can transform ad-hoc and intuitive decisions to data driven. Erstwhile misinformed decisions are now supported by concrete numbers and metrics.

Analytics has become an important part of organizations with it playing a major role in their corporate strategies. Thus, it is essential to understand the steps of inculcating and assimilating it in a business.

a)   Gathering and encapsulating structured and unstructured data from several sources to a common database is a standard start. Combining financial data with with other key operating data is one of the core steps as it unifies the data across the stakeholders of the business for analysis.
b)   Backward integration is a common route in integrating analytics into an organization. Defining the critical business problems and major decisions made frequently helps identify the current optimal usage of information in decision making.
c)   Data management is the next step which revolves around segregating key relevant information from the large mixed pool of data. Structuring that to support different functions of a business is a vital and initial part of the process.
d)   Train the employees on the application along with detailed orientation programs. Inadequacy of comprehension of the details of the software and technology would not produce the desired results and better decision making for the organization.

The process can take a few months / years depending on the size of the organization but within that time, a supportive and encouraging environment needs to be created. Inducing analytics into business functions such as finance requires constant change and a shift from the status- quo. Despite the technical challenges and time blocks such as gathering and accumulating the data, a shift in working style may not be supported by a lot of managers/workers. Leaving one's comfort zone is always a challenge and same is the case over here. Analytics leverages data and information for decision making in contrast to gut and intuition which feels like a loss in power for the managers. The integration can have high financial as well as opportunity costs associated with it, that however reduces in the long run because increased efficiency and accuracy resulted through the analytics approach saves money for the firm. Not just costs but there is also a change in timelines, policies that affect different roles across a company.

Most businesses can benefit from financial analytics given its advantages and despite its challenges but at the same time it is very essential that the basic ordinance of the organization like timed financial reports, data gathering and other simple metrics are on course.

FINANCIAL ANALYTICS USING EVIEWS

AUTHOR BIO

Parul Kumar

Parul Kumar is an Assistant Professor at Vivekananda Institute of Professional Studies and has submitted her thesis on Foreign Portfolio Investors and Stock Market Relation at School of Management Studies, IGNOU. Her area of specialisation is Finance and Capital Markets. She is an expert of analytical tools and software and has trained several academicians and corporate employees through her Faculty and Management Development programs. Her expertise is in the area of Data Analytics, Data Modelling and Financial Analytics.

1. INTRODUCTION

This chapter explains how econometric modeling is done on financial data in EViews. One of the most prominent methods of analyzing time series or financial data is Regression. The Chapter starts with explaining in brief about time series followed by the concept of Autocorrelation, Stationarity and Heteroskedasticity. The next section details a step by step guide for conducting Regression Analysis along with various model fit tests.

2. TIME SERIES

A time series is defined as a set of quantitative observations arranged in chronological order.

Statistically every observation is a random realization of a stochastic process.

- Time Series data may be related to their own previous data (such as autoregressive & moving average terms)
- They may be subject to deterministic trends, seasonality, cycles etc.
- Time series may also contain linear or non- linear trends which can be traced out through closed supervision of time series plot.
- In multivariate context, they may have cross-correlations. (For example, Foreign Portfolio Investment in India for the month of January will affect share prices not only in the month of January but may affect the share prices of February and coming months as well.)

To analyze the Time series, few important checks have to be done i.e.

a) Check for Normality (Jarqe Bera, Skewness and Kurtosis)
b) Check for Stationarity of the data (ADF and PP)
c) Check for Autocorrelation (Correlogram)

These are basic requirements before using any econometric tool on the time series. Even after finalizing the model for the research, these tests are conducted to check the model fit. In other words, the regression model is tested for normality (usually ignored), absence of serial correlation (Breusch Pagan LM Test & Correlogram), and possible heteroskedasticity (Breusch Pagan Godfrey Test). When the model stratifies all these tests, only then it is considered fit and can be generalized to the whole population. All these are explained in detail in this chapter by way of EViews.

EViews is a powerful tool for conducting various types of statistical and econometric tests. It has a built in powerful tool kit to estimate the times series models ranging from simplest to the most complex ones. The first step is to create a file known as workfile in EViews.

3. CREATION OF EVIEWS WORKFILE

EViews can create a new file in which all the variables are entered by the researcher himself. But this is the long process, as each perspective must be defined by the researcher. Hence the easy way is to open the Excel or SPSS file in Eviews is by way of "Foreign Data File".

Steps for Opening an Excel or SPSS file in EViews:

a) Go to File » Open » Foreign Data as Workfile.
b) Select the Excel or SPSS file and press Open.
c) A new dialog box appears giving details of the file.
d) There is by default Cell range selected in "Predefined Range" as Sheet 1. This can be changed by using the drop-down arrow next to it.
e) Next, even the Custom Range can be set. Here Start Cell and the End cell can be selected as per the requirement of the researcher. Then click Next.
f) In the next step, column headers and their details are given. Again, they can be changed according to the requirement.
g) Then Click Finish. The work-file would open.
h) Now the values of the series can be viewed by clicking the desired series with the help of Ctrl key. This will highlight the series selected. To view the contents of these, click View » Open as One Window » Open Group or double click on either of the highlighted series and click Open Group.
i) The values will now appear in a worksheet that is similar to an Excel worksheet.
j) These values should be checked to see whether they agree with the values in the range selected.
k) If it is sure that the data entered into the EViews work-file has been done correctly, then the work-file should be saved. File » Save As. (In the dialog box that appears to enter the name of the file "Financial Analytics". One need not to enter .wf1 as EViews automatically adds this to all of its work-files.
l) Now the file can be opened from File » Open » File name.

There are three basic requirements of the Time series i.e. Normality, Stationarity and Autocorrelation.

A. NORMALITY

Normality means that the data is normally distributed or evenly distributed over the period. For researches involving primary data, condition of normality must be met. Although in case of financial data, which is mostly secondary, this condition is not mandatory. This is because economic or financial data depends upon economic happenings and is of technical nature, thus it is not necessary that the time series data should be stationary before building of regression or other econometric models. This can be checked by way of Skewness, Kurtosis and Jarque Bera Statistics.

Skewness is a measure of symmetry of the histogram. Skewness of a symmetrical distribution, such as the normal distribution, is zero. If the upper tail of the distribution is thicker than the lower tail, skewness will be positive.

Kurtosis is a measure of the tail shape of a histogram. Kurtosis of a normal distribution is three. If the distribution has thicker tails than the normal distribution, its kurtosis will exceed three.

The Jarque Bera statistic tests whether a series is normally distributed. Under the null hypothesis of normality, the Jarque Bera statistic is distributed Chi-square with 2 degrees of freedom.

In EViews, normality statistics is estimated by Descriptive Analysis of data or the series.

Steps for Descriptive Analysis

- Go to Quick » Series Statistics » Histogram & Stats.
- Put the series name.
- Press Ok and the output is shown.

Exhibit: Descriptive Analysis

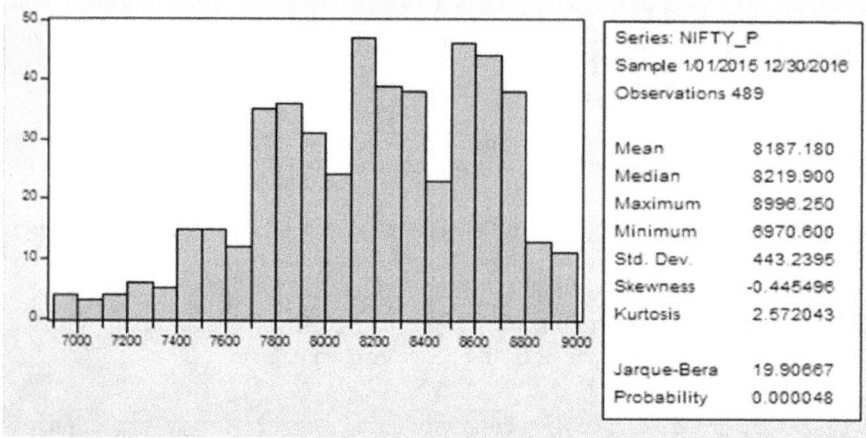

Series: NIFTY_P	
Sample 1/01/2015 12/30/2016	
Observations 489	
Mean	8187.180
Median	8219.900
Maximum	8996.250
Minimum	6970.600
Std. Dev.	443.2395
Skewness	-0.445496
Kurtosis	2.572043
Jarque-Bera	19.90667
Probability	0.000048

It can be seen from the histogram that the series is not stationary. Skewness is also less than zero i.e. it is negatively skewed. Kurtosis is less than three thus indicating non-stationary series. Jarque-Bera Statistics is also beyond the limits and its p value is less than 0.05 and therefore fails to reject the alternate hypothesis that series is not stationary.

B. STATIONARITY

A time series is strictly stationary if all the moments of its probability distribution (such as mean, variance, skewness, kurtosis and others) are invariant over time. However, in practice researchers are more concerned about weakly stationary process (also called covariance stationary or second-order stationary). A time series is called weakly stationary, if it's mean variance and auto-covariance remain the same no matter at what point of time they are measured. A non-stationary series is also called a unit root process. A stationary time series will tend to return to its mean and fluctuations around this mean will have broadly constant amplitude. Therefore, researchers can have a reliable prediction about its future behavior. On the other-hand one cannot make any such prediction about the behavior of a non-stationary time series which may have time varying mean or variance. If one studies a non-stationary series for a specific time-period, any statistic obtained on its basis is applicable for that particular period of time only and it cannot be generalized. Stationarity is checked by Unit Root Tests.

UNIT ROOT TESTS

The unit root tests can be studied in two categories based on the null hypothesis involved.

- Testing the null hypothesis of unit root against the alternative hypothesis of stationarity. This category includes Augmented Dickey –Fuller (ADF) test and Phillip Perron (PP) test.
- Testing the null hypothesis of stationarity against alternative hypothesis of unit root. The most popular test in this category is KPSS test.

Augmented Dickey –Fuller (ADF) test is most frequently used test of unit root. It is based on simple logic. A non-stationary process has infinite memory as it does not show decay in a shock that takes place in the process. Every random shock carries away the process from its earlier level not to return back again unless another random shock pushes it towards its previous level.

STEPS FOR CONDUCTING UNIT ROOT TEST

a) Go to Quick – Series Statistics – Unit Root Tests.
b) Enter the Series name (i.e. variable name).
c) Press Ok. Figure 4 would appear.
d) Select the Name of the test in "Test Type".
e) Select the level in Test for "Unit root in".
f) Select Intercept in "Include in test equation".
g) Press Ok. The output is shown.

Result of the ADF is shown. Here one has to read t–statistics and the probability. If p value is less than 0.05 then the series or variable is stationary, otherwise one will fail to reject the null hypothesis that the series has unit root and is not stationary.

When the variable is non-stationary repeat this test with Option "trend and intercept", if found stationary then it can be interpreted as trend stationary. In this case, series has to be detrend, or explicitly trend has to be included in the model.

If again the series turns out to be non-stationary, test has to be repeated with "1st Difference". If found stationary the variable is difference -stationary or integrated of Order 1 i.e. I (1).

Exhibit: ADF Result

Augmented Dickey-Fuller Unit Root Test on NIFTY_P			
Null Hypothesis: NIFTY_P has a unit root			
Exogenous: Constant			
Lag Length: 0 (Automatic - based on SIC, maxlag=17)			

		t-Statistic	Prob.*
Augmented Dickey-Fuller test statistic		-2.015640	0.2801
Test critical values:	1% level	-3.443496	
	5% level	-2.867231	
	10% level	-2.569863	

*MacKinnon (1996) one-sided p-values.

Augmented Dickey-Fuller Test Equation
Dependent Variable: D(NIFTY_P)
Method: Least Squares
Date: 06/12/17 Time: 20:53
Sample: 1/01/2015 12/30/2016
Included observations: 489

Variable	Coefficient	Std. Error	t-Statistic	Prob.
NIFTY_P(-1)	-0.016499	0.008186	-2.015640	0.0444
C	134.8885	67.11719	2.009746	0.0450

R-squared	0.008273	Mean dependent var	-0.198160
Adjusted R-squared	0.006237	S.D. dependent var	80.40485
S.E. of regression	80.15371	Akaike info criterion	11.60985
Sum squared resid	3128789.	Schwarz criterion	11.62700
Log likelihood	-2836.609	Hannan-Quinn criter.	11.61659
F-statistic	4.062805	Durbin-Watson stat	1.848581
Prob(F-statistic)	0.044386		

C. AUTOCORRELATION

The correlation between the current observations of a time series with its own past observations at time lag $k = 1....n$ is called autocorrelation of order $k(\rho_k)$. The non-stationary series will show very high autocorrelation close to 1; which, unlike a true AR process, does not show an exponential decay. Partial autocorrelation of order k is the correlation between the current observations of a time series (y_t) and a past observation y_{t-m} after removing the impact of all the intermediate observations. There is the Graphical way to analyze the serial correlation or autocorrelation in the series. There is an econometric tool also to detect the serial correlation in the regression model. Graphically serial correlation in series can be detected by Correlogram and by LM Test serial correlation can be detected in model.

CORRELOGRAM

Steps for Correlogram in EViews:

1. Go to Quick » Series Statistics » Correlogram.
2. Put the series name.
3. Then select the Level i.e. Correlogram at Level or 1st difference or 2nd difference.
4. Select the Number of lags to include (in case of monthly data 12 maximum lags, in case of daily data maximum 5 or 7 lags should be chosen).
5. Press Ok and the output is shown.

When the Autocorrelation (AC) and Partial Correlation (PAC) charts are within the lower and upper bounds, then the series is termed as Stationary. Also probability can be seen, which is greater than 0.05, hence the series is stationary. The chart when the series is non-stationary, have both AC & PAC outside the bounds and even the probability is less than 0.05.

Regression models cannot be based on the non-stationary series, thus first they have to be made stationary only then they can used. Stationarity can be achieved either differencing or taking the lag or taking the square root or natural log of the series. The choice of transformation depends upon the type of data.

Exhibit: Correlogram of a Stationary & Non-Stationary Series

Correlogram of NIFTY_R

Date: 06/12/17 Time: 19:13
Sample: 1/01/2015 12/30/2016
Included observations: 489

Autocorrelation	Partial Correlation		AC	PAC	Q-Stat	Prob
		1	0.065	0.065	2.0538	0.152
		2	-0.050	-0.055	3.2924	0.193
		3	0.051	0.058	4.5554	0.207
		4	-0.036	-0.046	5.1819	0.269
		5	-0.106	-0.095	10.742	0.057
		6	-0.048	-0.042	11.867	0.065
		7	0.048	0.048	13.008	0.072
		8	-0.050	-0.053	14.266	0.075
		9	0.038	0.048	14.981	0.091
		10	0.018	-0.012	15.142	0.127
		11	-0.038	-0.035	15.871	0.146
		12	0.013	0.017	15.952	0.193
		13	-0.025	-0.034	16.262	0.235
		14	-0.023	-0.013	16.526	0.282
		15	-0.032	-0.028	17.054	0.316
		16	-0.023	-0.031	17.313	0.366
		17	-0.032	-0.030	17.837	0.399
		18	-0.043	-0.043	18.771	0.406
		19	0.025	0.016	19.087	0.451
		20	0.024	0.010	19.390	0.497

Correlogram of NIFTY_P

Date: 06/12/17 Time: 19:52
Sample: 1/01/2015 12/30/2016
Included observations: 489

Autocorrelation	Partial Correlation		AC	PAC	Q-Stat	Prob
		1	0.983	0.983	475.90	0.000
		2	0.965	-0.079	934.70	0.000
		3	0.947	0.046	1378.2	0.000
		4	0.929	-0.055	1805.5	0.000
		5	0.912	0.031	2217.8	0.000
		6	0.897	0.079	2618.1	0.000
		7	0.885	0.035	3008.1	0.000
		8	0.871	-0.054	3386.4	0.000
		9	0.858	0.049	3754.8	0.000
		10	0.845	-0.052	4112.4	0.000
		11	0.830	-0.002	4458.8	0.000
		12	0.817	0.031	4795.1	0.000
		13	0.804	-0.034	5121.0	0.000
		14	0.791	0.021	5437.0	0.000
		15	0.778	0.010	5744.0	0.000
		16	0.767	0.017	6042.8	0.000
		17	0.757	0.023	6334.0	0.000
		18	0.747	0.022	6618.6	0.000
		19	0.739	0.039	6897.7	0.000
		20	0.731	-0.020	7171.0	0.000

After the basic requirements of Time series or it can be said that Regression is met, and then the next step is to build the regression equation.

4. BUILDING A REGRESSION MODEL IN EVIEWS

Building a regression model involves specifying a time series equation. In EViews specifying an equation is very easy. The steps are as follows:

Steps:

a) Open workfile saved or new file.

b) In the main menu, select Object » New Object » Equation and click OK (OR) select the series which are to be included in the equation in the sequence of dependent followed by the independent series. Then right click & Open » as Equation.

c) The Equation Estimation box opens, with the series selected or you can write the name of the series.

d) Series are written in the sequence of dependent followed by the constant and then the independent. Here the method of estimation can also be changed from the pre –selected one i.e. LS – Least square (NLS and ARMA) to other as per the researcher requirement.

e) Then press Ok and the output would be shown.

If you want to keep a permanent record of the equation that you have estimated, then click "Name" button above the output. Enter the name in the dialogue box that you wish to give to the equation and then click OK. The name will appear in the work-file with an equal-to sign in front to indicate it is an equation.

Exhibit: Final Output of Estimation

Dependent Variable: FPI_NI
Method: Least Squares
Date: 06/13/17   Time: 23:30
Sample (adjusted): 1/04/2000 12/30/2016
Included observations: 4220 after adjustments

Variable	Coefficient	Std. Error	t-Statistic	Prob.
C	194.6598	12.77141	15.24183	0.0000
NIFTY_R	17.90418	8.434378	2.122762	0.0338

R-squared	0.001067	Mean dependent var		195.3544
Adjusted R-squared	0.000830	S.D. dependent var		829.7228
S.E. of regression	829.3782	Akaike info criterion		16.27970
Sum squared resid	2.90E+09	Schwarz criterion		16.28271
Log likelihood	-34348.17	Hannan-Quinn criter.		16.28077
F-statistic	4.506118	Durbin-Watson stat		1.247340
Prob(F-statistic)	0.033832			

EViews also allows to re-estimate an equation. To do this, click the "Estimate" button above the output. Equation Specification dialog box appears again containing the equation that you entered the first time. You can now change the name of any variable or change the sample that you are using.

The output from EViews can be divided into three parts. The first part shows the name of the Dependent Variable, the time and date when the equation was estimated, the Sample used and the number of observations. The second part shows the estimated values of the intercept and the coefficient of independent variable along with the t statistics and p values.

Now if level of significance (α) is 5% then the decision rule to choose between the hypotheses concerning the intercept is:

Reject H0: $\beta 0 = 0$ if $p < \alpha = 0.05$

Thus, the conclusion when $p < \alpha$ will be, fail to reject the alternate hypothesis i.e. the intercept is not 0. Similarly, for the independent variable p value, i.e. it is less than 0.05, thus independent variable is significantly impacting the dependent variable.

The third part of the output shows the measures that suggest the model fit and the collective impact of the variables/series on dependent variable. The two measures of the proportion of the variation or variance which the model explains are found in the top left-hand corner. The F statistic and its probability or p value are found in the bottom right hand corner. R square shows the variation in the dependent variable that is explained by the independent variable. R square value of greater than 0.06 or 60% is considered a good model. Although there is caution i.e. *high R-squared does not necessarily imply that the model is a good or useful one,* this may be because the independent variables are insignificant which may be due to presence of multicollinearity. The F statistics along with the probability determine whether all the independent variables together or collectively impact the dependent variable or not. If p value is less than 0.05, it can be concluded that independent variables are collectively significant in impacting the dependent variable.

5. ANALYZING THE MODEL FIT OR RESIDUAL DIAGNOSTICS

One way of determining whether a model fits the data well is to examine the residuals from the estimated equation which are automatically stored in "resid". If the model is a good fit then these residuals should satisfy the assumptions concerning the error terms. Graphs can be drawn of the residuals or the Histogram and Stats command can be used with these values. Also, the presence of Serial Correlation, Heteroskedasticity and Multicollineriaty is to be checked to finally consider the model for generalization and further evaluation. View menu shows Actual, Fitted, Residual; the Coefficient diagnostics in which Variance Inflationary Factor for

Multicollinearity is there and then the residual diagnostics, in which Correlogram, Normality, Serial Correlation and Heteroskedasticity can be seen.

A. NORMALITY

Here we check the normality of the residuals of the model. Although in the financial data the criteria of normality is mostly ignored. It is analyzed by way of a histogram and descriptive statistics of the residuals, including the Jarque-Bera statistic for testing normality. If the residuals are normally distributed, the histogram should be bell-shaped and the Jarque-Bera statistic should not be significant. The Jarque-Bera statistic has a distribution with two degrees of freedom under the null hypothesis of normally distributed errors.

Steps:

- Select View » Residual Diagnostics » Histogram » Normality Test.
- The output is shown.

The histogram depicts that the residuals are not normal and are negatively skewed. Even the probability value of Jarque bera is less than 0.05, thus rejecting the null hypothesis that the residuals are normally distributed.

Exhibit: Descriptive Statistics of Residuals

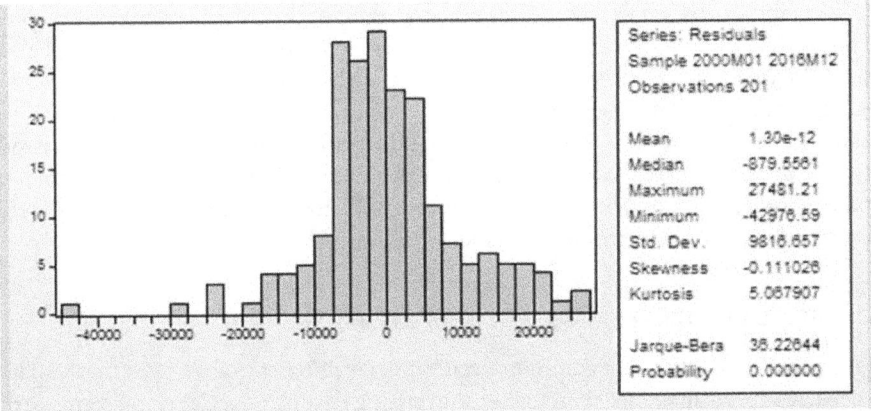

B. RESIDUAL GRAPH

EViews also provides with a graph which shows the actual or Y values, the fitted or estimated values and the residuals or differences between the actual and estimated values. To obtain the set of values and/or their graph after obtaining the regression output Click View » Actual, Fitted, and Residual. There if values are required then click on Table and if Graph is required as shown in the figure, then click Graph.

Exhibit: Actual, Fitted and Residual

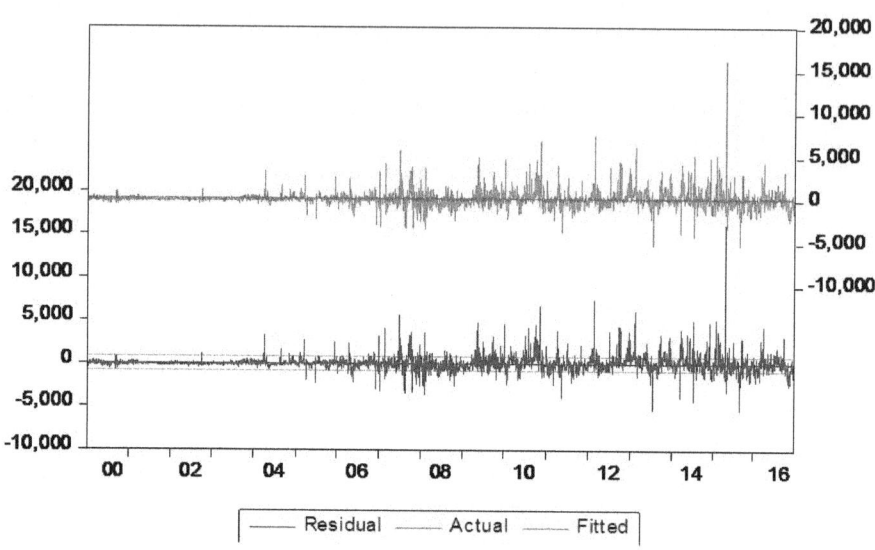

From this diagram, it can be found that where the large residuals have occurred as these indicate when the model has failed to accurately predict dependent variable. Here it can be seen that variance of the residuals seems to have increased. Graph also helps in analyzing whether there are patterns in the errors that are supposed to be scattered in a random way. Typical patterns one can see may be a saw tooth pattern caused by seasonal effects. Or the errors trending up or down for part of the period which would suggest that the model is not stable. Another pattern i.e. a curved pattern more like a parabola can also be seen, which would show that a non-linear equation needs to be fitted to the model.

c. SERIAL CORRELATION OR AUTOCORRELATION

Serial correlation is a common occurrence in time series data because the data is ordered (over time); it is therefore not surprising that neighboring error terms turn out to be correlated. Serial correlation violates the standard assumption of regression theory that error terms are uncorrelated. If the serial correlation is not treated, it leads to biasness in the coefficients and reported standard errors and t-statistics become invalid. As discussed earlier there is correlogram to detect the presence of correlation, like wise there are two more statistics to test this i.e. Durbin Watson and Breusch Godfrey LM Test.

a) Durbin Watson

EViews automatically computes the DW statistic and includes it in every equation object. To test the hypothesis of no serial correlation, compare the reported DW statistic to a table of critical values. The value nearer to two indicates the absence of serial correlation.

b) Breusch Godfrey LM Test

The null hypothesis is that there is no serial correlation in the residuals up to the specified lag. The steps of performing this residual test are as follows:

- Click View » Residual Diagnostics » Serial Correlation LM Test.
- Select the number of lags. Here one needs to specify the highest order of serial correlation one would like to test. If testing for first order serial correlation, specify lags = 1.
- Click Ok and result would be shown.

Exhibit: Serial Correlation Test

Breusch-Godfrey Serial Correlation LM Test:

F-statistic	695.4433	Prob. F(1,4217)	0.0000
Obs*R-squared	597.4157	Prob. Chi-Square(1)	0.0000

Test Equation:
Dependent Variable: RESID
Method: Least Squares
Date: 06/14/17   Time: 01:14
Sample: 1/04/2000 12/30/2016
Included observations: 4220
Presample missing value lagged residuals set to zero.

Variable	Coefficient	Std. Error	t-Statistic	Prob.
C	-0.016403	11.83433	-0.001386	0.9989
NIFTY_R	-1.586108	7.815746	-0.202938	0.8392
RESID(-1)	0.376316	0.014270	26.37126	0.0000

R-squared	0.141568	Mean dependent var	2.26E-13
Adjusted R-squared	0.141161	S.D. dependent var	829.2799
S.E. of regression	768.5235	Akaike info criterion	16.12753
Sum squared resid	2.49E+09	Schwarz criterion	16.13204
Log likelihood	-34026.09	Hannan-Quinn criter.	16.12913
F-statistic	347.7217	Durbin-Watson stat	2.138246
Prob(F-statistic)	0.000000		

The top panel reports the test statistics in two versions: the F-statistic and the Chi-squared statistics (either one is fine) along with the associated p-values. The bottom panel provides additional information of the auxiliary regression that is carried out to create the test statistic. Since only first order serial correlation is tested, there is only one residual lag in the auxiliary regression. The null hypothesis of no serial correlation is rejected in favor of the alternate hypothesis i.e. there is presence of serial correlation in the model.

D. HETEROSKEDASTICITY

This is a very general test for non-constancy of the variance of the residuals. If the residuals have non-constant variance then ordinary least squares is not the best estimation technique i.e. weighted least squares should be used instead. Nothing rules out the possibility that both heteroskedasticity and serial correlation are present in a regression model. Serial correlation has a larger impact on standard errors and efficiency of estimators than heteroskedasticity. However, heteroskedasticity may be of concern especially in small samples. In addition, in many financial time series, the conditional variance of the error term depends on past values of the error term. This is also known as autoregressive conditional heteroskedasticity (ARCH). Heteroskedasticity can be tested by Breusch Pagan Godfrey, White & ARCH Test. The one caveat is that, when testing for heteroskedasticity, residuals should not be serially correlated. Any serial correlation will generally invalidate tests for heteroskedasticity. It thus makes sense to test for serial correlation first, correct for serial correlation, and then test for heteroskedasticity. Most commonly, both heteroskedasticity and autocorrelation of unknown form can be corrected using the HAC Consistent Covariance (Newey-West).

a) Breusch Pagan Godfrey Test

This test regresses the squared residuals on the original regressors by default.

Steps:

- View » Residual Diagnostics » Heteroskedasticity Tests.
- By Default Breusch Pagan Godfrey is selected.
- Click Ok.

Exhibit: Result of Breusch Pagan Godfrey Test

Heteroskedasticity Test: Breusch-Pagan-Godfrey

F-statistic	0.037846	Prob. F(1,4218)	0.8458
Obs*R-squared	0.037864	Prob. Chi-Square(1)	0.8457
Scaled explained SS	0.866434	Prob. Chi-Square(1)	0.3519

b) White Test

White's (1980) test is a test of the null hypothesis of no heteroskedasticity against heteroskedasticity of unknown, general form. The test statistic is computed by an auxiliary regression; where model regress the squared residuals on all possible (nonredundant) cross products of the regressors. White also describes this approach as a general test for model misspecification, since the null hypothesis underlying the test assumes that the errors are both homoscedastic and independent of the regressors, and that the linear specification of the model is correct. Failure of any one of these conditions could lead to a significant test statistic. Conversely, a non-significant test statistic implies that none of the three conditions is violated.

Steps:

- View » Residual Diagnostics » Heteroskedasticity Tests.
- Click on White from the Test Type.
- One may choose to include or exclude the cross terms. If you do not wish to include the cross term, uncheck the box "Include White cross terms". The test will simply be carried out with only the squared terms.
- Click Ok and result is shown.

Exhibit: Result of White Test

Heteroskedasticity Test: White

F-statistic	0.023317	Prob. F(2,4217)	0.9770
Obs*R-squared	0.046667	Prob. Chi-Square(2)	0.9769
Scaled explained SS	1.067866	Prob. Chi-Square(2)	0.5863

Thus, based on the test statistics, null hypothesis of homoscedasticity is failed to be rejected. In other words, the error term is homoscedastic and standard errors should not be adjusted.

c) ARCH Test

The ARCH test is a Lagrange multiplier (LM) test for autoregressive conditional heteroskedasticity (ARCH) in the residuals (Engle 1982). This heteroskedasticity specification was motivated by the observation that in many financial time series, the magnitude of residuals appeared to be related to the magnitude of recent residuals. ARCH does not invalidate standard LS inference. However, ignoring ARCH effects may result in loss of efficiency.

It is also possible that the regression has ARCH terms in the data studied above. To test for this, let's perform an ARCH LM test. The null hypothesis is that there is no ARCH up to order lags in the residuals.

Steps:

- View » Residual Diagnostics » Heteroskedasticity Tests.
- Select ARCH under the Test Type.
- Select the number of lags. In this case it is two.
- Click Ok.

Exhibit: ARCH Test Result

Heteroskedasticity Test: ARCH

F-statistic	6.535440	Prob. F(2,4215)	0.0015
Obs*R-squared	13.03975	Prob. Chi-Square(2)	0.0015

The figure shows the results of the ARCH LM test and again probability of either F Statistics of the Chi-square should be seen. Here again the null hypothesis of no ARCH is rejected, thus it concludes that residuals suffer from this specific form of heteroskedasticity.

Addressing Heteroskedasticity and Autocorrelation: Robust Standard Errors

EViews provides built-in tools that allows to adjust standard errors for the presence of both heteroskedasticity and autocorrelation of unknown form (HAC – Newey – West).

Steps:

- Click on the Equation box.
- The Equation Estimation box opens-up. Click Options.
- Under the Coefficient Covariance matrix drop-down menu, choose HAC (Newey-West).
- Click OK.

EViews re-estimates the equation, this time adjusting the standard errors for heteroskedasticity and autocorrelation of unknown form. As expected, the estimated coefficient values do not change. But, the adjusted standard errors (and associated t-statistics) are different from the original regression. Now this model is again checked for serial correlation and heteroskedasticity. The result shows that the residuals of the model are not serially correlated and error terms are homoscedastic.

Exhibit: Output After Newey Test

Dependent Variable: FPI_NI
Method: Least Squares
Date: 06/14/17   Time: 01:50
Sample (adjusted): 1/04/2000 12/30/2016
Included observations: 4220 after adjustments
HAC standard errors & covariance (Bartlett kernel, Newey-West fixed
   bandwidth = 10.0000)

Variable	Coefficient	Std. Error	t-Statistic	Prob.
C	194.6598	23.60164	8.247722	0.0000
NIFTY_R	17.90418	7.373190	2.428281	0.0152

R-squared	0.001067	Mean dependent var	195.3544
Adjusted R-squared	0.000830	S.D. dependent var	829.7228
S.E. of regression	829.3782	Akaike info criterion	16.27970
Sum squared resid	2.90E+09	Schwarz criterion	16.28271
Log likelihood	-34348.17	Hannan-Quinn criter.	16.28077
F-statistic	4.506118	Durbin-Watson stat	1.247340
Prob(F-statistic)	0.033832	Wald F-statistic	5.896548
Prob(Wald F-statistic)	0.015212		

E. MULTICOLLINEARITY

Multicollinearity exists when two or more of the predictors in a regression model are moderately or highly correlated. Unfortunately, when it exists, it can wreak havoc on the analysis and thereby limit the research conclusions that can be drawn. Some econometricians argue that if the model is otherwise OK, just ignore it. It can be noted that there will always be some degree of multicollinearity, especially in time series data. Some of the common methods used for detecting multicollinearity include:

- The analysis exhibits the signs of multicollinearity - such as estimates of the coefficients vary from model to model.
- The t-tests for each of the individual slopes are non-significant ($P > 0.05$), but the overall F-test for testing all the slopes are simultaneously 0 is significant ($P < 0.05$).
- The correlations among pairs of predictor variables are large.
- Looking at correlations only among *pairs* of predictors, however, is limiting. It is possible that the pairwise correlations are small, and yet a linear dependence exists among three or even more variables. That›s why many regression analysts often rely on what are called **variance inflation factors** (*VIF*) to help detect multicollinearity.

Variance Inflation Factors (VIFs) are a method of measuring the level of collinearity between the regressors in an equation. VIFs show how much of the variance of a coefficient estimate of a regressor has been inflated due to collinearity with the other regressors. There are two forms of the Variance Inflation Factor: centered and uncentered. The centered VIF is the ratio of the variance of the coefficient estimate from the original equation divided by the variance from a coefficient estimate from an equation with only that regressor and a constant. The uncentered VIF is the ratio of the variance of the coefficient estimate from the original equation divided by the variance from a coefficient estimate from an equation with only one regressor (and no constant). VIF values that exceed 10 are generally viewed as evidence of the existence of problematic multicollinearity. This happens for $R^2_j > 0.9$ (explain auxiliary regression), so large standard errors will lead to large confidence intervals.

The easiest ways to remove multicollinearity are:

- Drop one of the collinear variables.
- Transform the highly correlated variables into a ratio or lag or difference.
- Collect more data i.e. may be a longer run of data or change frequency of the data.

Steps:

- Click View » Coefficients Diagnostics » Variance Inflationary Factor.
- The output is shown in the figure.

Exhibit: VIF Output

Variance Inflation Factors
Date: 06/15/17 Time: 22:43
Sample: 2000M01 2016M12
Included observations: 201

Variable	Coefficient Variance	Uncentered VIF	Centered VIF
C	8267324.	16.29542	NA
NIFTY_RET	27407.68	2.659083	2.625228
S_P_RET	363722.3	13.32598	13.29094
CHANGE_MCAP	975.5180	1.166532	1.163652
EXRATE_R	191078.2	1.698287	1.678805
MSCI_BRICS_R	41845.34	4.901062	4.888124
CMR	163550.1	15.33639	1.168727
CPI_US	444890.2	5.794559	1.596669
FOREX	8.90E-05	1.392612	1.221761
IIP	41.05881	2.866443	1.218934
LIBOR	197049.6	3.348588	1.665334
MCSI_R	480492.2	19.54204	19.52853

As it can be seen in the output, in two figures the value is greater than 10. This indicates the presence of multicollinearity. The variables S&P 500 return (S_P_RET) and Morgan Stanely Capital Index return (MCSI_R) are related to each as shown by the VIF values. This relationship is true also as S&P is the part of MCSI and hence there is out to be collinearity between them. In the presence of this the regression results get affected thus it is necessary to remove this multicollinearity. As mentioned earlier there are three ways to remove this, in the present case one can opt for transformation as it is not possible to drop any of the variables from the study. Thus, any one of them can be either differenced or taken at lag and then possible multicollinearity will be removed.

Hence by correcting these inefficiencies in the model as well as in the series, one will arrive at the effective regression model which is suitable for forecasting as well as generalizing it for the population i.e. the years beyond the sample.

6. CONCLUSION

This chapter focused on the financial analytics by way of Time series. Regression analysis has been conducted here to understand the financial analytics. The first and foremost criteria for the application of Regression are to check whether the series or variables are stationary and not autocorrelated. After confirming these, the next step comes is building of regression model i.e. equation defining dependent & independent variables. EViews is a great tool for analyzing time series data. After running the equation in the EViews, the results are checked for normality, presence of autocorrelation, heteroskedasticity and multicollinearity. If the model satisfies all the criteria then it is deemed fit for representation.

Section

HR Analytics

'In God we trust, all others bring data'

- W. Edwards Deming

'Without data, you are just another person with an opinion'

- W. Edwards Deming

HR ANALYTICS

AUTHOR BIO

Shweta Shrivastava

Shweta Shrivastava is a Research Scholar at Faculty of Management Studies, University of Delhi and is working in the domain of Human Resources and Organisational Behaviour. Her interest areas are rewards, incentives and organizational commitment. She has 7 years of corporate work experience with organizations like Mercer Consulting, Everonn Education and HCL Technologies. She is a Post Graduate in Human Resources from Loyola Institute of Business Administration, Chennai and a Graduate in Commerce from Shri Ram College of Commerce, University of Delhi.

1. UNDERSTANDING HUMAN RESOURCE MANAGEMENT

PEOPLE AS RESOURCES

An organization requires three basic resources to operate – land, labor and capital. Land is required to set up a physical workspace or a factory for production of goods and services. Capital provides the much-required financial support to an organization which ensures survival of the organization. Labor or the people resource refers to the people or employees who work in the organization and create services or goods. The cumulative knowledge, creative abilities, talents and aptitudes of the workforce of an organization constitutes people resources. This human resource helps an organization to keep the business afloat as without skilled and capable people, an organization cannot seek to function, perform, innovate or become a profitable venture – which is the aim of every business venture. Through human resource, all other resources can be created or improved and therefore be 'managed'.

In the competitive working environment that exists today, an organization needs to be agile, take smart business decisions and rise above competition. It also needs to have access to important information, possess management expertise, entrepreneurship acumen etc. Each of these is only possible when the organization is armed with required skills and competencies, has an able leadership and can motivate its employees to perform well. Since an organization is only as strong as its people, the combined intellect, experience and expertise of its employees gives an organization its competitive edge and a distinct character. Therefore, in today's business ecosystem, human resource is the most strategic asset that an organization can possess.

To effectively manage its people resources, organizations need to focus on policies and practices which govern how people are managed and developed. A strong focus on employee focused practices leads to multiple and enhanced long term advantages for organizations such as higher profitability, reduced turnover, greater innovation, higher product / service quality, lower production costs etc. Through employee centric practices, an organization can ensure that its employees are engaged and committed to their work.

The following section showcases the way human resource management adds value to the organization.

A. HUMAN RESOURCE MANAGEMENT

Human Resources Management (HRM) is also referred to as labor management, employee-employer relations, personnel administration, industrial relations etc. HRM can be described as an approach that an organization adopts to manage its people resources who contribute to the goals and objectives of the organization. It aims to create an environment or a system where employees perform to their maximum potential for the betterment of the organization and for their own advancement. It perceives employees as assets of the company and ties their performance and attitudes with organizational goals and objectives.

HRM differs from the earlier used approach of personnel management, which was more administrative in nature and had an operational focus. Personnel management considered employees as cost centers as compared to HRM which considers the strategic value of employees as assets. HRM provides solutions and insights into a wider range of organizational issues and considers employees as strategic assets. It intends to ensure that skilled employees are attracted, motivated and retained in the organization, leading to its superior performance. There has been significant research that documents a strong link between human resource practices and strategic organizational outcomes such as organizational performance and a strong culture. Thus, the focus and attention towards employee focused practices has also increased.

Sound human resource management serves a multitude of purposes:

- Well-crafted and implemented policies and practices can motivate employees.
- It helps organizations to perform well, outperform competition and achieve financial success.
- It also leads to effective utilization of organizational resources.
- It ensures individual development of employees through enhanced performance and skill development.

Human resource management adds value to an organization through its managerial and operative functions which lead to effective management of human resources. Managerial functions include the function's responsibilities of planning, organizing, directing and controlling people resources in the organization.

a) Managerial Functions

- **Planning:** This is one of the most crucial responsibility area of managing human resources. The human resource function should be able to predict or forecast the workforce requirement of an organization based on the trends in the market to fulfil the manpower needs. It also entails catering to specific needs of organizations. For instance, ensuring the availability of project managers with an advanced certification in project management for a client project is the responsibility of the human resource management function.
- **Organizing:** The multiple and often contrasting manpower needs of various departments in an organization should be met through proper organization of people resources at the appropriate time. Deployment of resources in simultaneous and successive projects without disrupting the workflow is one aspect of organizing human resources. For example, a statistician might be assisting two simultaneous projects in finance and marketing departments and may then be required to undertake an international project soon thereafter.

- **Directing:** An organization performs well when its employees put in their collective effort towards achieving the goals of the organization. This happens when they are assigned responsibilities to be fulfilled. The directing function ensures that employees are appropriately directed to perform and the tasks are successfully executed. It is a crucial aspect of eliciting contribution of employees towards the organization. Leadership through effective coaching and mentoring are crucial to enable employees to reach their own, as well as organizational goals.
- **Controlling:** To ensure that actual performance of employees is in conformity with the planned performance, human resource functions need to be verified and checked. Controlling helps to ensure that there is no deviance from initial directions. Performance reviews help managers to monitor performance of employees and to chart out development plans for them.

b) Operative Functions

The operative functions of human resource management pertain to the specific activities that are performed by it throughout the life cycle of an employee; starting from his recruitment to his separation from the organization. In conjunction with the managerial functions stated above, human resources management procures, develops, compensates, and integrates the human resource with work situations and work environment.

- **Procurement:** One of the main functions of human resources is to ensure that appropriate employees are deployed for appropriate jobs at the appropriate time. Therefore, human resource management must see to it that employees with required skills and competencies are hired when required. Procurement function deals with the planning for manpower requirements, selection and placement, their induction and on-boarding, transfer, redeployment and separation. Planning forms the backbone of all procurement activities, failing which organizational goals can remain unachieved.
- **Development:** Once employees are hired by an organization, they may be required to undergo certain mandatory process and functional training. The development ensures that employees are armed with knowledge necessary to perform their job. It also includes other development related aspects such as coaching, counselling and mentoring, performance appraisal and management which help to increase the performance potential of an employee. Doing this not only leads to the increase the current performance of an employee but also makes them ready for any future roles that they may assume in the organization. For instance, succession planning helps to create a pipeline of trained resources for critical positions in an organization. It involves identification of skills and competencies for a position (e.g. CEO

position), identification of potential candidates and then training the person for fulfilling those responsibilities. It is interesting to note that succession planning alludes not only to the procurement function of human resource management but also to development function while being founded on the operative function of planning. Therefore, it can be said that the functions of human resource management should be viewed as overlapping and in integration and not in isolation.

- **Compensating:** In return for their contribution to the organization, employees should be rewarded adequately. This requires establishing job descriptions, pay grades and salary structures, job analysis, securing information about compensation through salary surveys etc. Employees require extrinsic compensation such as cash and benefits. Employees also seek intrinsic compensation in the form of meaningful jobs, independence in work, development opportunities. To be effective, organizations need to pay their employees appropriately and create employee friendly reward systems.

- **Integration:** Another function of human resource management is to ensure proper relation between employers and employees. A cordial and cooperative relationship leads to a productive work environment in an organization. Therefore, it is important that employees' morale remains high, intra and interpersonal relations between individual employees and work groups are pleasant, grievances are redressed on time, fair disciplinary procedures exist and that quality of work life is maintained and improved. Encouraging the creation of a collaborative, productive and high-performance culture is a responsibility of human resource management.

Through all its functions, human resource management is concerned with all kinds of people requirements in an organization. It transcends through all teams, departments, functions, geographical locations etc. Owing to its all-encompassing and holistic nature, its applications is not limited only to human resource department and therefore it becomes the responsibility of all managers in an organization. It adopts a 'soft' approach towards employees and considers them as valuable assets who need to be developed and nurtured in return for their commitment, engagement and performance in the organization.

c) Human Capital Management

In recent years, Human Capital management or HCM has become a popular term in the management domain. The concept of HCM has its foundation in HRM as it seeks to analyze, measure and evaluate how people policies and practices create value for businesses. In other words, while both HRM and HCM consider employees as crucial resources, HCM is more quantitative in nature. It works on the premise that human beings as assets must bring some incremental and quantifiable value to businesses through their skills, knowledge and abilities. Due to such advantage, organizations ought to invest in these assets, nurture and develop them. Therefore, in the domain of analytics, the term HCM is found to be more frequently used as it discusses the value that employees bring to the organization. Software solutions provided by major global organizations use the term HCM as opposed to HRM.

The following section discusses the concept of HR analytics and the way it adds to business operations.

2. UNDERSTANDING ANALYTICS

In the fast-changing work environment that exists today, it is very important for organizations to be aware of changing demands and requirements of their customers, employees and other stakeholders as well the market and economic conditions. Therefore, decision making in business has become more complex and multi-faceted. Most organizations collect, report and use large volumes of data during their business operations. Such data can pertain to employees (their names, age, work experience, qualifications, performance), stock markets, financial performance of peer companies etc., sales and marketing of products and services such as use of demographic data to create marketing campaigns etc. In this electronic age, social media platforms such as websites, blogs, social networks etc. provide a lot of information to organizations about their products and services. In an agile environment, understanding trends and patterns of such data can help business managers take logical decisions and improve the quality of products and services. It also helps to identify current and past performance, to monitor current progress towards organizational goals and to create strategies to identify areas for growth.

Use of analytics in business is growing steadily especially due to the wide spread prevalence of structured and unstructured big data in companies. Analytics can be defined as a study of data using statistical and operations analysis to aid decision making. Many organizations world-wide are resorting to analytics to get strategic insights into business and to take informed fact-based decisions. Analytics helps to integrate large volume of data that organizations have and use it diligently for business decisions. Without the use of analytical techniques, handling such large data can be a challenge for organizations. Hence, organizations today use a variety of techniques to simplify and synthesize data. Analytics, therefore, turns data into actionable insights and helps to unearth information, facts, trends and patterns that were unknown earlier. It enhances decision making by providing insight into alternate options available to management and estimates of risk.

Business Intelligence, a term often used in the context of analytics, differs from analytics as it enables decision making based on what happened in the past. It aids problem identification and resolution also. It includes activities like:

- Simple reporting of what has happened in the past on a business front.

- Understanding why something happened. It requires structured thought process and an understanding of business. It involves exploring data to find relationships and patterns.
- Preparing dashboards and reports which are interactive and summarize key business metrics to help understand the current state of operations. It provides real-time information about business.

In contrast, analytics uses past data and historical trends to predict future which is one of its key objectives and requires problem solving skills, statistical and analytical abilities.

Stemming from the broad spectrum of uses of analytics, three main types of analytics have gained popularity in the corporate world today. They are descriptive statistics, prescriptive analytics and predictive analytics. These three types have varied applications and advantages.

a) **Descriptive statistics** refers to characteristics of data through a summary of the data points and is one of the oldest form of analytics. For instance, a count of how many times a web user visited a website is a descriptive statistic. In terms of statistics, descriptive statistics also includes details of data such as its mean, standard deviation, variance etc. Such details help to understand the nature of data.

b) **Predictive analytics** is the most widely used form of analytics. It uses data analysis techniques such as predictive algorithms to predict what is about to happen next. Its advantages in planning ahead for future possibilities has made it a popular technique in many organizations, especially in field of consumer behavior. For instance, purchase recommendations made by online sale portals (e.g. Amazon, Flipkart) to users is done based on their past purchases. Such recommendations have led to almost 30% of Amazon's sales.

c) **Prescriptive analytics** is a newer technique in comparison to the other two. While predictive analytics answers 'what will happen next', prescriptive analytics provides to solutions to what needs to be done keeping likelihood of future possibilities into consideration. It uses techniques such as big data, contextual analysis and computing power to answer such questions.

Analytics is being extensively used in various industries such as retail, banking, e-commerce, and a host of service based industries such as airlines, hospitality etc. An example can be the application of analytics by retail organizations to understand customer behavior, loyalty programs, promotional offers and discounts etc. Banks have been seen to use analytics to segment customers using analytics based on credit usage, risk profiles etc. A reason for such wide spread adoption of analytics in these industries is the availability of large volumes of data which can be subjected to a variety of techniques for understanding and interpretation. There are other areas of management such as Human Resources where use of analytics is at a nascent stage and is hoped to become widely used in years to come.

A. ANALYTICS IN HUMAN RESOURCES

An arena where analytics has now made it foray is human resources. In the recent years, it has been so due to the increasing realization about the power of analytics in the domain, the increasing pressure from boards and management of organizations to measure and quantify people related decisions, and a general recognition amongst human resource professionals to boost their business acumen. Along with this, research has also indicated a strong connection between analytics and business performance of organizations. Due to these reasons, several organizations have adopted analytics to make their people centric decisions more sound and robust.

It is interesting to note that HR analytics, even though the name suggests, is not just about HR! Rather, it is about people related measures which both the managers of the organization and the HR consider important for the success of the organization.

HR Analytics (also known as Data Analytics, People Analytics or Workforce Analytics) simplifies critical human resource challenges for organizations by using business analytics techniques such as data mining, predictive analytics, contextual analytics and others. Predictive analytics, which helps to predict future outcomes, replaces managerial intuitions with data driven decision making. It identifies underlying patterns in data sets by using algorithms and helps to predict needs and performance of an organization and its employees. In the domain of HR, it can be successfully used in many functions to take appropriate decisions.

B. WHY IS HR ANALYTICS IMPORTANT?

For long, HR has been thought of as a 'cost center' and its actual contributions to organizations have often been looked at with skepticism when compared with other functions in organizations such as Finance, Sales, Operations, Quality etc. The main reason behind this perception is that these functions can *quantify* their performance and value addition. HR department is a custodian of vast amount of data such employees' age, academic qualification, gender, tenure, experience, skills, trainings undertaken, performance ratings etc. However, the department has been known to contribute qualitatively and to rely more on intuition and less on the objective power of metrics. Owing to this inherent nature of the de Therefore, the need for HR is to quantify and measure the impact of human capital decisions on the business, and that of organization's decisions on human capital. This is where HR Analytics plays a crucial role as it helps the function become more *quantitative* rather than *qualitative*.

HR analytics adds value to organizations as it leads to data-based decision making, brings rigor to HR activities and helps to prioritize them based on their positive impact and return on investment to the organization. By resorting to objective evidence based analysis of information and facts, HR Analytics helps to do away with the subjectivity in HR decisions. The quantification of HR is not as easy as it for other functions. For instance, the measurement of motivational impact of a performance management system or the effectiveness of training is not easy as it involves measurement of employee attitudes and behavior, which varies significantly based on situations and conditions.

Owing to its low reliance on data driven decision making in the past, HR has fallen short of metrics and analytical models to correctly assess the effectiveness of its practices that are needed to add value to the organization. However, with the increased focus on analytics in the domain of HR, this seems to be changing. Enterprise Resource Planning (ERP) and HR Information systems (HRIS) have helped to standardize information and have made access to such information easier. A lot of organizations are now steadily adopting array of tools and techniques, ranging from HR metrics and predictive analysis to improve the decision making in the people aspect of business.

The key initiatives that HR needs to take that are 'quantitative' in nature are:

- Understand financial systems and strategies to become more data driven and to align people measures to organizational outcomes.
- Communicate in business terms to showcase a better linkage to organizational performance.
- Use storytelling and visualization in its communication as these two techniques have become popular in the business world. They help to explore, explain and engage a larger audience.

Thus, HR Analytics intends to eliminate the 'guesswork' from people management by connecting it with business outcomes.

c. WHAT DOES IT DO?

The core purpose of HR Analytics is to improve both individual and organizational performance. It helps organization decide on which activities resources should be deployed and where they should not be deployed. Thereby, HR Analytics helps organizations channel their efforts in the right direction and to improve the credibility of the HR function.

HR Analytics achieves these by answering critical questions relating to the workforce and by providing crucial insights into aspects such as recruitment, workforce requirements, effective deployment and utilization of employed resources, performance, succession planning, attrition, employee satisfaction etc. By analyzing trends, setting productivity goals and effectively monitoring them, analytics empowers organizations to minimize risks and to take speedy decisions such as:

- How productivity can be improved
- Which employees are best suited for a job or project
- Whether the organization is well staffed to meet organizational goals in the next few years
- How individuals, teams, departments or organization is performing against its preset key performance indicators
- What are the skill gaps and how those can be filled
- How can employees be engaged in their work

D. HR Metrics vs. HR Analytics

It is crucial to understand the difference between HR Metrics and HR Analytics. Exhibit 1 shows this difference.

Exhibit: Understanding Metrics and Analytics

	Metric	Analytics
Perspective	Inside	Outside-In
Value	Low	High
Time context	Past	Past, Present & Future
Nature	Informational	Strategic

Very often the terms metrics and analytics are used interchangeably. However, there is a difference between the two terms. When data is gathered with no specific reason in mind, it is referred to as measurement. Metrics refers to gathering, counting, tracking or presenting past data for specific reasons. For instance, the number of defective items produced in a manufacturing unit in a month or the number of outstanding performers in a performance cycle or other information in the repository of Human Resources such as age, academic qualification, gender, tenure, experience, skills, trainings undertaken, performance ratings etc. are example of metrics. It refers to tangible internal information about the organization that provides a basic insight to the management. Such details are low in terms of value as they can be conveniently gathered.

The next step is to take judicious and informed decisions based on these metrics and the organizational goals. To take appropriate decisions, organizations also need to be aware of both past as well present data about internal and external aspects of operations such as labor market, economic condition, business growth, competition etc. Such holistic information is then used to gain valuable insights, predictions and optimizations. Therefore, it can be said that HR Analytics makes intelligent use of metrics to predict future outcomes accurately and to create value. It leads to creation of information that can be used to make crucial business decisions.

An example that helps to differentiate and understand the two concepts of metrics and analytics is that of gender diversity. The number of women in leadership positions is a metric that is one of the indicators of gender diversity in an organization. However, the reason (why) behind a low or high level of women incumbents and ways to bridge it, is a part of analytics.

Diversity refers to feature of a mixed workforce that provides a wide range of abilities, experience, knowledge, and strengths due to its heterogeneity in age, background, ethnicity, physical abilities, political and religious beliefs, sex, and other attributes. The list shown below mentions measures of diversity keeping its definition into consideration:

Exhibit: Measures of Diversity in an Organization

- Perception of consistent and equitable treatment of employees
- Extent of meaningful jobs to handicapped employees
- Compliance with technical requirements of affirmative action
- Compliance with fair employment practices
- Degree of objectivity and neutrality in rewards and promotions
- Percent of non-traditional workers in applicant pool
- Nontraditional workforce promotion rate
- Nontraditional workforce turnover rate
- Average age of workforce

Source: Ulrich, D. (1997). Measuring human resources: an overview of practice and a prescription for results. Human Resource Management, 36(3), 303-320

3. BALANCED SCORECARD APPROACH

The balanced scorecard approach is based on the stakeholder model that states that for any business to thrive it must focus on three stakeholders:

a) **Investors:** This focuses on measures such as profitability, market value and others that indicate towards the financial performance of the organization to ensure that investors' interest is protected and maintained.

b) **Consumers:** A firm's growth and survival are dependent on the consumers that it serves. This is reflected by measures such as the market share of the product or service, customer retention, customer satisfaction and other measures which focus on consumers.

c) **Employees:** When employees of an organization feel protected and valued by the organization, they contribute towards the success and performance of their organization.

A balanced focus on each of the three stakeholders helps organizations to achieve sustained performance and growth. Out of the three, employees are the toughest to measure as the associated measures are less defined and rigorous, and hence less focused upon in general. Employee related measures can be split into three categories:

a) **Productivity:** This refers to the measure of output per employee and may include transaction per employee (financial productivity), production per employee (manufacturing output), revenue per employee (retail productivity) etc. Such measures are more objective, straightforward and standard across industries.

b) **People:** One of the most crucial and difficult aspects of employee measures, this relates to gauging how employees respond to policies/practices of the organization, whether they feel committed to the organization and if they feel satisfied with their jobs etc. Measures such as absenteeism, turnover, attrition, grievances are indicators of employees' attitude towards the organization. Few organizations conduct satisfaction surveys and engagement surveys to understand how their employees feel about their jobs/organization and whether they feel engaged in their jobs. An example of Engagement Survey is the Gallup Q^{12} Survey which measures employees' engagement and enthusiasm towards their jobs and is linked to key organizational outcomes such turnover, profitability and safety.

Exhibit: Gallup's Q12 Survey

The Q^{12} statements are:

Q00. (Overall satisfaction) On a 5-point scale where "5" is extremely satisfied and "1" is extremely dissatisfied, how satisfied are you with (your company) as a place to work?

Q01. I know what is expected of me at work.

Q02. I have the materials and equipment I need to do my work right.

Q03. At work, I have the opportunity to do what I do best every day.

Q04. In the last seven days, I have received recognition or praise for doing good work.

Q05. My supervisor, or someone at work, seems to care about me as a person.

Q06. There is someone at work who encourages my development.

Q07. At work, my opinions seem to count.

Q08. The mission or purpose of my company makes me feel job is important.

Q09. My associates or fellow employees are committed to doing quality work.

Q10. I have a best friend at work.

Q11. In the last six months, someone at work has talked to me about my progress.

Q12. This last year, I have had the opportunity at work to learn and grow.

Source: Gallup, Inc.

People measures also include organization's awareness, and its employees' knowledge and competencies as it helps to deploy them in appropriate roles. It is also immensely helpful for strategic activities like succession planning and business continuity planning.

c) Process: From a people perspective, it is also important to understand how employees perceive the systems and the people component of business operations. For instance, at AT&T, a manager's salary increments and scorecard is calculated using his subordinates' response regarding leadership and diversity in their business. Other processes which are crucial to be perceived in a positive light by employees are equity and fairness in organizational practices, learning, shared mindset etc.

4. HR ANALYTICS: SOME EXAMPLES

Organizations are steadily moving towards the application of analytics in the field of HR. Below are examples of three multinational organizations which used analytics to improve some aspect of people management.

CASE 1: PIONEERING THE CAUSE OF ANALYTICS AT GOOGLE

Google is an organization that is known to have used analytics to strengthen various processes and that culture now also covers human capital management. The organization has created a people analytics team that works to identify most impactful people management practices by analyzing employee related issues and matters. This people analytics team workers directly with the Vice President of the organization. A representative of the analytics team works in each of the major HR functions. Google has also established a 'Pi-Lab' (People and Innovation Lab) which conducts applied experiments to determine the best approach to managing people based decisions. For instance, based on an experiment conducted by the Pi-Lab that aimed to find the correct portion of food for employees, the company started to stock 20 cm plates besides 30 cm plates. This encouraged employees to eat small and healthy sized meals. Such initiatives are a testimony of their seriousness towards the cause of analytics. They have used analytics for a variety of people related actions, for instance:

a) **Leadership Project:** 'Project Oxygen' was a research driven program that focused on identification and ranking of leadership attributes of managers. It was named so as it proved itself to be a lifeline for the organization by providing crucial insight into employees' expectations from their managers. This was done by correlating phrases, words from praises and complaints in performance reviews, feedback surveys from employees and nominations for Top Manager awards. These comments were then coded to identify patterns and then results were synthesized to identify 'Eight Habits of Highly Effective Google Managers' that were deemed requisites by employees. What emerged from this project was that employees at Google wanted their managers not just to possess technical knowledge but also to counsel and guide them through one-on-one discussions and personalized feedback. Technical expertise emerged as the last of the eight important traits of a manager – a revelation, since it had been considered a pre-requisite trait of a manager for many years. Instead, employees seemed to prefer managers who were accessible, showed interest in their lives and careers and provided solutions to problems. These results were incorporated into training programs, coaching and individual performance review sessions which led to improvement in the performance and perception of managers.

b) **Algorithm based hiring and retention:** Under Project Janus, Google has incorporated analytics in the recruitment process where they re-assess profiles of rejected candidates in each job family to detect profiles of good candidates that they may have missed. By revisiting such profiles, many potential performers have been hired and has thus increased the quality of hiring process. A retention algorithm has been incorporated by Google to flag employees who are likely to leave the organization. It enables them to use personalized retention plans such employees. This contrasts with traditional organizations that use managers' evaluation and feelings to highlight such employees which make it a subjective process that may prove to be inaccurate.

c) **Collaboration:** Google has been known for its culture of innovation which has been a strategic focus of the management of the organization. Their belief is that employees become innovative when they collaborate, discover with each other and have fun at work place. Since their analytics suggest this, their workplace designs are especially focused on this aspect of employee behavior. For example, they also track the time employees spend in collaborating with their colleagues in café lines. A survey suggested that lunch time needed to be extended by three to four minutes in order so that employees can collaborate with new people but do not end up wasting time either. Therefore, their workplaces are designed to consist of an informal culture with opportunities for employees to discuss and collaborate.

CASE 2: ACCENTURE'S USE OF CONTEXTUAL ANALYTICS

Accenture used contextual analytics in its recruitment process and thus made it more efficient. Contextual analytics refers to an analysis of text to understand its meaning, characteristics, the context of historical and structural setting etc. It also provides insight into the intentions of the author and the purpose that was set out to be achieved by choosing certain words and leaving out others.

Accenture used this form of analytics to hire 20,000 employees in its technology unit in India from a giant pool of 300,000 applications. The mammoth task of interviewing each of these many applicants, could have led to an elaborate and time-consuming process, thereby leading to poor quality of hired resources. Therefore, in collaboration with a technology partner, Accenture developed tools of contextual analytics. The steps taken are shown below:

a) Identify 'renege' candidates: The renege probability was identified to filter out those applicants who were likely to forego the job offer. This was done based on certain attributes of candidates that were identified through the text in the application of candidates. Such elimination helped the organization focus on those applicants who had better chances of joining the organization post selection.

b) Ascertain a 'High-Quality Hiring Index': The purpose of analytics is to help an organization achieve its goals. Accenture aligned the two by developing a High-Quality Hiring Index. The index signifies the characteristics of a good performer based on the needs and requirements of Accenture for their technology business. The index was matched with the probability of hiring for these employees. The ones with a higher probability were then interviewed with the positives outcomes such as efficient recruitment (selection of right candidates) and time (reduction by 60%) and cost saving through prioritization of interviews.

This exercise at Accenture was done using where specific tools that were created on the principles of contextual analytics. It helped them to create a meaningful engagement for the recruitment team and to make their recruitment process systematic and impactful.

Case 3: Application of Talent Analytics Software at PepsiCo

PepsiCo is a global organization with an employee strength of around 300,000 employees and operates in 80 countries. Due to its enormous size, ensuring uniformity of people centric decisions became a daunting task for the organization. Different cultures, working styles and management ways, the human resources systems appeared to be disconnected and 'scattered'. Therefore, it failed to provide an organizational level insight into people operations to the management. This led to the organization embarking on a journey to synthesize the operations around the world using big data and cloud services – '1000 steps to analytics'. The intent was to transform the way human resources were managed by digitizing it using analytics software so that there would be just one source of information for everyone at the organization in all geographies.

It turned out to be an uphill task as there were stakeholders in different parts of the world and diversity of language and regulations only added to the enormity of the task. The organization, to standardize the human resource management system, also standardized the definitions of roles across regions and countries. Harmonization of job titles and organization structure allowed managers at PepsiCo across the globe to view consistent and standardized information and take more informed decisions. It eventually helped PepsiCo to undertake organization wide strategic projects such as workforce planning, comparison of CEO pay ratios, calculation of gender pay ratio etc. It would not have been possible without an integrated view of the historic data pertaining to the organization and then combining it with the organizational objectives.

5. HR ANALYTICS: SUCCESS FACTORS

Successful and efficient use of HR analytics in an organization requires three knowledge and skills of three main areas:

a) **Knowledge of human resources as a domain**: Recruitment, selection, rewards, performance management, training & development are few crucial aspects of human resource management. Organizations prefer to hire post graduates in the domain of Human Resources, Personnel Management or Industrial Relations to handle people related activities in the organization as they have detailed knowledge of the various facets of the function. Human Resource managers need to have basic knowledge of these functions, as without it application of analytical techniques may not yield an impactful result.

For instance, an Accounts Manager may not be able to frame a sound performance management process which enables employees to achieve a superior performance, identifies the training needs of employees and has the desired impact of motivating them as well. Once the process of performance management has been designed, the effectiveness can be monitored using the various techniques of data analysis.

b) **Statistics**: Only with a data driven HR function can an organization monitor the impact of its HR decisions and further take informed decisions. Techniques and tools of statistics can be immensely useful in the domain of human resource in areas such as satisfaction surveys, compensation surveys, training feedback evaluation, HR accounting and budgeting etc. For instance, statistics can be used in determining the relationship between employee satisfaction and HR practices and help the organization focus on practices which have a greater impact on satisfaction of employees. For proper interpretation of data, specialist skills in statistics are immensely useful. Statistical techniques can be used in usual reporting as well. As organizations are realizing the importance of statistics in the domain of HR, there has been an increase in customized courses in statistics that focus on increasing analytical capabilities of HR professionals.

c) **Consulting**: Acting as internal consultants can help Human Resource professionals to influence and convince decision makers about their suggestions and action ideas. Data can be used to impact the analytical mind set of the multiple stakeholders involved in a decision to adopt a certain set of recommendations. For example, adoption of a learning management system to better monitor performance of new sales personnel requires the buy in of both the human resource specialists as well as leaders from the sales team. For such tasks, ability to recognize patterns of problems and the ripple effects on related organizational problems helps to increase the effectiveness of analytics in organizations. Communication skills are also of immense use in such situations. Other than problem solving skills and the ability to extract meaning out of data, a consultant approach also helps to create an understanding of how organizational issues are deeply connected to each other. HR can gauge the impact of their decisions by the effect they have on other related functions as well as there are several stakeholders from multiple functions that make implementation of a change possible.

The People Analytics team at Google consists of three categories of employees. The first set is Human Resource Professionals who are experts in areas such as Compensation and Benefits or are Human Resource Generalists. The second set comprises of employees with a background of strategy consulting as they are able to delve deep into organizational problems and often have a holistic understanding of business operations. The third group consists of employees who have advanced degrees such Doctorates or Masters degree in various related areas. Such employees contribute by running experiments or carrying researches to augment data driven decision making at the organizations.

6. HR ANALYTICS: SOME INHIBITORS

There are organizations that are realizing the long term strategic benefits of adopting HR Analytics. Despite the increasing focus, there are reasons why it has not become a norm. The following section describes those reasons:

a) While many organizations use metrics, they are often inconsistent and differently employed across organizations. For example, return on investment on training is a metric that is found to be difficult to quantify by many organizations. However, the measurement of this return is very different and unique to each organization. It depends on the strategic objectives of the organization behind a training program. For behavioral changes, such as increased leadership capability, calculating return will be difficult as compared to monitoring increase in sales performance.

b) Sometimes, data on people measures does not integrate with the overall business and operational measures as the two are considered to work in silos. Managers do not see the benefit of analytics in HR. An example can be the case of the manufacturing department which tracks the 'production output' of employees whereas the HR department reports 'people related' data. As the respective leaders concentrate on their own areas and data, it creates a gap in their integration and so HR analytics becomes a low priority. However, analytics can lead to better management in this case too. For instance, the productivity measures of the manufacturing staff can be used to identify training needs, which can further boost the production output of employees. To remedy this, metrics need to be tied to the overall business performance and aligned with organizational strategies.

7. CRUCIAL ANALYTICS TECHNIQUES

The core purpose of Human Resource Analytics is to link people related measures with the organizational outcome measures. In other words, the intent is to ensure that the processes of human resource management are aligned with the organizational goals. Analytics provides the link between the drivers of employee performance and business results. Statistical tests are run on softwares such as SPSS or Excel etc. and the results provide insights to management.

The most effective statistical techniques are:

a) Correlation: For a better understanding of business operations, organizations often want to know if certain phenomenon is related. For example, if there is a relationship between organizational rewards and employees' motivation levels or between job satisfaction and employee engagement. This kind of insight comes from correlation analysis which states whether a relationship exists at all between two phenomena. An example of correlation is shown in the Exhibit where there is a moderate correlation between job satisfaction and employee engagement.

Exhibit: Correlation between Job Satisfaction and Employee Engagement

	Job Satisfaction	Employee Engagement
Job Satisfaction	1.000	0.601
Employee Engagement	0.601	1.000

b) Multivariate analysis: This is a set of analytical techniques that analyses more than two variables at a time. It focuses on dependence (e.g. multiple regression) or interdependence relationships (e.g. factor analysis). For example, an organization may want to determine the relationship between its job satisfaction of its employees with their engagement levels. For this, it will need information from employees about their satisfaction from different factors such as benefits, job, cooperation, team, company policies etc. It will also try to assess the engagement levels of employees. It will make use of multivariate technique of regression. Such analysis helps to understand issues such as:
- Does job satisfaction have an impact on employee engagement?
- What factors of job satisfaction have the most significant impact on engagement of employees?

c) Comparison of means / t-tests: At times, an organization may want to know if employees' perception towards some practice or a policy varies due to another factor (say, age, gender, experience etc.). To gain such insights, comparison of means or t-tests are performed on data. It can further help organizations to frame policies to suit the preferences of workforce.

The above-mentioned tools and techniques are just to provide a glimpse of how data analysis can provide a better understanding of how effective HR programs and policies are. The selection and application of tools and techniques varies on the basis of the questions for which the organizations are seeking answers.

8. MAJOR SERVICE PROVIDERS OF
HR ANALYTICS SOFTWARE

Organizations specialising in HR analytics softwares had initially begun with specialised domain focussed solutions like a learning management system or an applicant tracking system. With the increase in the need for businesses to have an integrated view of human resources, these organizations progressed to providing integrated solutions that cater to solutions in all domains. The advent of cloud computing has led to availability of analytical solutions on hand-held computing devices in the form of applications.

With the increase in adoption of analytics by organizations, the number of organizations that provide software for the purpose has also gone up. Today, there are specific and specialised software for analysing data related to different facets of human resources as well as huge vendors which provide a bigger basket of integrated analytical solutions. Some of the key software providers for HR solutions are:

a)   SAP has a core HR cloud based application called SAP SuccessFactors Employee Central provides an employee record and HR related platform but also integrates the entire work experience and has seen an increase in the number of users of EmployeeCentral in the last year. SAP also has two software called SuccessFactors Workforce Analytics and SuccessFactors Workforce Planning which specifically work on retention prediction and workforce planning respectively.

b)   (Automatic data Processing) ADP's human capital management provides both integrated and specialised softwares for HR analytics. It provides a cloud based solution to various areas such as core HR through Workforce Now and payroll services through RUN.

c)   Oracle is one of the leaders in Human Capital Management solutions. It has cloud based solutions for core HR, talent acquisition and talent management. Oracle HCM cloud is can be used in conjunction with other applications such as ERP and EPM, which makes it a more convenient and holistic its use.

d)   Workday also provides integrated solutions in the form of Workday Human Capital Management Suite which acts as a unified source of all information pertaining to Talent Management, Benefits Management, Recruiting and HR Management.

9. CONCLUSION

As the business world becomes more dynamic and complex, taking appropriate decisions becomes more and more difficult. The importance of employees' intellect, competencies and skills in making organizations successful cannot be emphasized more. It is of utmost importance that the intuition based qualitative approach of people management be replaced by one that is led by a more objective, fact-based and quantified approach. Leading organizations in the world have adopted the same and are gained from it. Analytics in the domain of HR has gained wide acceptance due its ensuing advantages which is reflected in the continuing growth of HCM vendors such as SAP, Workday, ADP etc. It will only enhance the importance of human resource management in making an organization an efficient and profitable venture.

Section

Analytics Software

MICROSOFT EXCEL

AUTHOR BIO

Havish Madhvapaty

Havish presently works as Head of Research with Traverse Strategy Consultants, a research and consulting start-up, where he leads a team of analysts, spearheading research work. He is a corporate and academic trainer in quantitative analysis, focusing on Advanced Microsoft Excel and SPSS. He has trained organizations such as Uber, ITC, Tata Motors, WIPRO and so on. He is active on the Microsoft community as an expert contributor. Havish has over 25 academic publications in national and international journals, and has acted as a reviewer for IGI Global. He is pursuing his Ph.D. in the area of experiential marketing. He has authored a book titled RENVOI: Business Management Cases. His research assignments have been featured regularly in BW|Businessworld, BW|Applause, BW|Education, IMPACT and so on.

Is this chapter for you?

The chapter is designed for intermediate users. It covers essential intermediate components of Excel and complex topics that are aimed at power users. Excel offers immense possibilities as the user explores more of its options. Even users with years of experience will find something newer, and more efficient ways of performing tasks.

Software Versions

The chapter is written for Microsoft Excel 2013 for Windows. Users of Excel 2016, Excel 2010, and Excel 2007 will also face no concerns as nearly all the information applies to other versions as well. The chapter only covers the standard desktop version of Excel 2013, and not the web or mobile version.

Conventions

Excel 2013 does not use a menu system. The context-sensitive Ribbon at the top consists of *tabs* (File, Insert, Page Layout, and so on). Tabs consist of *commands* which are arranged in *groups*.

Example: Home » Font » Font Size

Some commands can be accessed by opening the *Dialog box launcher*.

Example: Home » Font » Font Settings

1. FORMULAS AND FUNCTIONS

A *formula* consists of a special code entered into a cell. The calculation performed returns a result, which is then displayed in the cell.

A. FORMULA ELEMENTS

A formula can consist of any of the following elements:

- Mathematical Operators
- Cell references
- Values or text
- Worksheet functions (such as SUM, AVERAGE, MIN, MAX etc.)

Exhibit: Examples of Using Formulas

=100+50	Adds 100 and 50. Returns the result 150.
=B1	Returns the value in cell B1.
=A1+B1	Adds the values in cells A1 and B1.
=SUM (A1:A12)	Adds the values in cells A1 till A12, using the SUM function.
=A1=A2	Compares values in the two cells. Returns TRUE if cells are identical, else FALSE.

Operators are symbols that indicate the mathematical operation the formula performs.

Exhibit: Operators Used in Formulas

Operator	Name
+	Addition
-	Subtraction
*	Multiplication
/	Division
^	Exponentiation
&	Concatenation
=	Logical comparison (equal to)
>	Logical comparison (greater than)
<	Logical comparison (less than)
>=	Logical comparison (greater than or equal to)

<=	Logical comparison (less than or equal to)
<>	Logical comparison (not equal to)

Multiple operators / combination of operators can be used as per the requirement.

Operator precedence is very important, else a result might appear, but it might be incorrect.

Exhibit: Operator Precedence in Excel Formulas

Symbol	Operator	Precedence
^	Exponentiation	1
*	Multiplication	2
/	Division	2
+	Addition	3
−	Subtraction	3
&	Concatenation	4
=	Equal to	5
<	Less than	5
>	Greater than	5

Parentheses is used to override the order of precedence. Expressions contained within parentheses are evaluated first.

Exhibit: Use of Parentheses to Change Order Precedence

Example	Result
=100*15-5	1495
=100*(15-5)	1000

Use of *functions* allow for simplification of formulas.

=(A1:A2:A3:A4:A5)/5
=AVERAGE(A1:A2:A3:A4:A5)

Formulas can be inserted using multiple techniques:

a) Type an equal sign (=) followed by the formula name.
b) Insert functions from one of the function categories.
   Insert » Formulas » Insert Function.
c) Hybrid formula entry: Write the formula name, followed by Ctrl + A.

Formulas can be edited in the following ways:

a) Double click inside a cell.
b) Press F2 to go into Edit mode.

*** **Pro Tip** ***
Shortcut to enter formulas: Shift + F3
Press Ctrl + Shift + U to expand formula window
Press Ctrl + ~ to show formulas.
Use function FORMULATEXT to get the entire formula as text.
Press Ctrl + [to show direct precedent cells.
Press Ctrl + Shift + {to show all precedent cells.
Press Ctrl +] to show direct precedent cells.
Press Ctrl + Shift +} to show all precedent cells.

B. Relative, Absolute and Mixed references

This refers to the address part of the cell.

Relative	A1
Absolute	$A$1
Mixed	$A1, A$1

*** **Pro Tip** ***
Press F4 to toggle between dollar signs.

Example: Using one formula that can be copied and pasted in all cells.

	A	B	C	D	E	F	G
1		Region	Sales	Growth			
2				5%	10%	15%	20%
3		North	1000	=$C3*D$2	———————————————→		
4		West	1500	↓			
5		East	2000				
6		South	2500	↓			

c. ERRORS

Errors will inadvertently happen. While the effort should be focused on avoiding errors altogether, knowledge of errors helps when they need to be addressed.

Exhibit: Common Errors

Error Value	Description
#DIV/0!	#DIV/0! The formula is trying to divide by zero. This also occurs when the formula attempts to divide by an empty cell.
#NAME?	The formula uses a name that Excel does not recognize.
#N/A	Occurs primarily when using VLOOKUP, and cell reference cannot be located.
#REF!	The formula refers to a cell that isn't valid. This can happen if the cell has been deleted from the worksheet.
#VALUE!	The formula includes an argument or *operand* (value or cell reference used to calculate result) of the wrong type.

*** Pro Tip ***

If the entire cell is filled with hash-mark (#) characters, the column is not wide enough to display the value.
Solution: Widen the column or change the number format of the cell.

---

2. CONDITIONAL STATEMENTS

SUMIF and COUNTIF are very useful. The former returns the sum of cells that meet a specified criterion and the latter returns the count of cells that meet a specified criterion.

The COUNTIF function, which is useful for single-criterion counting formulas, takes two arguments:

range:	The range that contains the values that determine whether to include a particular cell in the count.
criteria:	The logical criteria that determine whether to include a particular cell in the count.

The SUMIF function, which is useful for single-criterion counting formulas, takes three arguments:

range:	The range that contains the values that determine whether to include a particular cell in the count.
criteria:	The logical criteria that determine whether to include a particular cell in the count.
sum_range:	Optional. The range that contains the cells you want to sum. If this argument is omitted, the function uses the range specified in the first argument.

Example: Count the number of cells greater than 1500; Calculate the sum of SALARY where REGION is North.

	A	B	C
1			
2		**REGION**	**SALES**
3		North	1000
4		West	1500
5		East	2000
6		North	2500
7		East	1000
8			**=COUNTIF (C3:C7, ">1500")**
9			**=SUMIF (B3:B7, "North", C3:C7)**

C8 will give the result "2"; C9 will give the result "3500".

These functions can be expanded to SUMIFS and COUNTIFS, which will use multiple criteria.

Exhibit: Excel Counting and Summing Functions

=COUNT	Returns the number of cells that contain a numeric value.
=COUNTA	Returns the number of nonblank cells.
=COUNTBLANK	Returns the number of blank cells.
=COUNTIF	Returns the number of cells that meet a specified criterion.
=COUNTIFS	Returns the number of cells that meet multiple criteria.
=DCOUNT	Counts the number of records that meet specified criteria; used with a worksheet database.
=DCOUNTA	Counts the number of nonblank records that meet specified criteria; used with a worksheet database.
=DSUM	Returns the sum of a column of values that meet specified criteria; used with a worksheet database.
=FREQUENCY	Calculates how often values occur within a range of values and returns a vertical array of numbers. Used only in a multicell array formula.
=SUBTOTAL	When used with a first argument of 2, 3, 102, or 103, returns a *count* of cells that comprise a subtotal; when used with a first argument of 9 or 109, returns the *sum* of cells that comprise a subtotal.
=SUM	Returns the sum of its arguments.
=SUMIF	Returns the sum of cells that meet a specified criterion.
=SUMIFS	Returns the sum of cells that meet multiple criteria.
=SUMPRODUCT	Multiplies corresponding cells in two or more ranges and returns the sum of those products.

Exhibit: Examples of COUNTIF Function

=COUNTIF (Data,15)	Returns the number of cells containing the value 15.
=COUNTIF (Data, "<0")	Returns the number of cells containing a negative value.
=COUNTIF (Data, "<>0")	Returns the number of cells not equal to 0.
=COUNTIF (Data, ">190")	Returns the number of cells greater than 190.
=COUNTIF (Data, AG1)	Returns the number of cells equal to the contents of cell AG1.

=COUNTIF (Data, "*")	Returns the number of cells containing text.
=COUNTIF (Data, "?????")	Returns the number of text cells containing exactly five characters.
=COUNTIF (Data, "sales")	Returns the number of cells containing the single word *sales* (not case sensitive).
=COUNTIF (Data, "*sales*")	Returns the number of cells containing the text *sales* anywhere within the text.
=COUNTIF (Data, "F*")	Returns the number of cells containing text that begins with the letter *F* (not case sensitive).
=COUNTIF (Data, TODAY())	Returns the number of cells containing the current date.
=COUNTIF (Data, ">"&AVERAGE(Data))	Returns the number of cells with a value greater than the average of the values.
=COUNTIF (Data,5)+COUNTIF(Data,-5)	Returns the number of cells containing the value 5 or –5

The basic IF condition is very versatile too, when coupled with the AND and OR operators.

Example: In column E2:E6, display "Bonus" if the following conditions are met:

a) Rating: 1-3
b) Division: CDFD
c) Salary: <50000

	A	B	C	D	E
1	Name	Salary	Division	Rating	
2	Dwayne	38261	HFD	3	
3	Johnson	82135	RAD	4	
4	Michael	24566	HFD	1	
5	Lyndon	15097	CDFD	5	
6	Baristow	38038	HFD	1	

Solution: In E2, write:
=IF (AND (OR (D2=1, D2=2, D2=3), C2 = "CDFD", B2<50000), "Bonus", "No Bonus")

A. Ignoring Errors When Summing

The SUM function does not work if the range to be summed includes any errors. For example, if one of the cells to be summed displays #N/A, the SUM function will also return #N/A.

The AGGREGATE function can be used to add values in a range and ignore the error cells.

=AGGREGATE (9,6, Data)
Here (9) specifies SUM, and (6) means ignore error values.

B. Summing The "top n" Values

Example: Add the 5 largest and the 5 smallest values.

	A	B
1	60	
2	83	{=SUM (LARGE (A1:A11, ROW (INDIRECT ("1:5"))))}
3	25	{=SUM (SMALL (A1:A11, {1,2,3}))}
4	46	
5	52	
6	50	
7	96	
8	94	
9	13	
10	72	
11	34	

B2 will give the result "405" and B3 will give the result "72".

*** Pro Tip ***
This formula uses an array formula. (Covered later in the chapter) The {} signs are not put manually, but are inserted automatically. Use Ctrl + Shift + Enter rather than Enter after writing the formula.

3. RANGES AND TABLES

A *cell* is a single element in a worksheet that holds a value, text, or a formula. The *address* consists of the column letter and row number. Example: X1

A group of cells is called a *range*. A range address is designated by specifying the upper-left cell address and the lower-right cell address, separated by a colon.

Exhibit: Example of Range Addresses

A48	A range that consists of a single cell.
B1:D1	Two cells that occupy one row and three columns.
G1:G613	613 cells in column G.
A1:D5	20 cells (four rows by five columns).
H1:H1048576	An entire column of cells; this range also can be expressed as H:H.
A9:XFD9	An entire row of cells; this range also can be expressed as 9:9.
A1:XFD1048576	All cells in a worksheet. This range also can be expressed as either A:XFD or 1:1048576.

A. Defining Range

To select range:

1. Use mouse button to drag and select the range.
2. Use Shift key along with navigation keys.

*** **Pro Tip** ***
Press Ctrl + Spacebar to select column.
Press Shift + Spacebar to select row.
Press F8 and then use cell pointer.
Press Ctrl and select with mouse to select non-contiguous cells.

Selecting special types of cells, such as only Formulas, Blanks etc. is also possible. There are two ways to do this:

a) Home » Find & Select » Go To Special
b) Press Ctrl + G and then select Special.

Range can be defined by a certain Name for easy reference.
Example: Calculate sum using Range Name

	A	B
	Month	**Sales**
1		
2	January	1000
3	February	1500
4	March	2000
5	April	3000
6	May	4000
7	June	5000
8		=SUM(DATA)

Here Cell B8 will give us the result 16500. B2:B7 has been defined as "DATA". To give the range name "DATA", you can use the following options:

a) Select the data and then write the name in Name Box, on the left side of the Formula bar.
b) FORMULAS » Define Name » Define Name

*** Pro Tip ***
Name Manager can be accessed using Ctrl + Shift + F3.
Name Manager contains a list of all defined name ranges.

B. CREATING TABLES

Creating a table in Excel is more than simply adding a cell border to data in cells. Table can be created in two ways:

a) Insert » Table
b) Ctrl + T

There are numerous advantages tables offer:

a) Automatically adds table references to Table, as well as Table Name.
b) Adds design to the Table.
c) Calculates formulas automatically.

To calculate automatic formulas without writing them,
Table Tools » Design » Table Style Options » Total Row

To rename Table,
Table Tools » Design » Table Style Options » Total Name

Example: Calculate the sum at the bottom of the table.

	A	B
1	**Month**	**Sales**
2	January	1000
3	February	1500
4	March	2000
5	April	3000
6	May	4000
7	June	5000
8		**16500**

None
Average
Count
Count Numbers
Max
Min
Sum
StdDev
Var
More Functions…

In cell B8, select SUM from the drop-down list that appears when you insert automatic formula.

Excel will create the following formula:
=SUBTOTAL (109, Table1[Sales])

*** **Pro Tip** ***
SUBTOTAL is a function, 109 is an enumerate argument that represents SUM.
Square brackets refer to "structured references" within a Table. When a Table is created, all column headings become "structured references". This means that these column names are automatically defined, and need not be defined manually. They can be accessed by writing the Table Number, followed by "[", then selecting the correct column reference.

4. LOOKUP FORMULAS

A *lookup formula* returns a value from a table by looking up another related value.

A. VLOOKUP

VLOOKUP is the most commonly used among different lookup formulas.

The VLOOKUP function looks up the value in the first column of the lookup table and returns the corresponding value in a specified table column.

VLOOKUP (lookup_value, table_array, col_index_num, range_lookup)

The VLOOKUP function's arguments are as follows:

lookup_value:	The value to be looked up in the first column of the lookup table.
table_array:	The range that contains the lookup table.
col_index_num:	The column number within the table from which the matching value is returned.
range_lookup:	Optional. If TRUE or omitted, an approximate match is returned. (If an exact match is not found, the next largest value that is less than lookup_value is returned.) If FALSE, VLOOKUP will search for an exact match. If VLOOKUP cannot find an exact match, the function returns #N/A.

Example: Calculate the Sales in Cell C8 for the Name given in C7.

	A	B	C	D	E
1	Id	Name	Sales		
2	801	Roger	2000		
3	612	Rafael	1700		
4	457	Andy	1400		
5	678	Andre	1800		
6					
7		Name	Andre		
8		Sales	*Insert VLOOKUP*		

The answer will be 1800.
The formula is:
VLOOKUP (C7, $A$1:$C$5, 3, FALSE)

Remember:
Ensure that $ signs are put in the right locations.
The column index number is NOT the actual column letter.
If the data you want as a result is NOT to the right of the lookup column, you cannot use VLOOKUP.

B. REVERSE **LOOKUP**

The MATCH and INDEX functions are often used together to perform lookups. The MATCH function returns the relative position of a cell in a range that matches a specified value. The syntax for MATCH is:

MATCH (lookup_value, lookup_array, match_type)

The MATCH function's arguments are as follows:

lookup_value:	The value you want to match in lookup_array. If match_type is 0 and the lookup_value is text, this argument can include wildcard characters * and?.
lookup_array:	The range being searched.
match_type:	(lookup_array must be in ascending order.) If match_type is 0, MATCH finds the first value exactly equal to lookup_value. If match_type is -1, MATCH finds the smallest value greater than or equal to lookup_value. (lookup_array must be in descending order.) If you omit the match_type argument, this argument is assumed to be 1.

The INDEX function returns a cell from a range. The syntax for the INDEX function is

INDEX (array, row_num, column_num)

The INDEX function's arguments are as follows:

array:	A range
row_num:	A row number within array
col_num:	A column number within array

Example: Calculate the Name in Cell C8 for whom the Sales is given in C7.

	A	B	C	D	E
1	Id	Name	Sales		
2	801	Roger	2000		
3	612	Rafael	1700		
4	457	Andy	1400		
5	678	Andre	1800		
6					
7		Sales	2000		
8		Name			

The answer will be Roger.
The formula is
=INDEX (F6:H10, MATCH (C7, C1:C5, 0), MATCH (B8, A1:C1, 0))

5. TIME AND DATE

Date and time functions enable the user to convert dates and times to serial numbers, which can then subsequently be used to perform operations.

A. How Excel deals with Dates and Times

Serial numbers are used to represent specific dates and times. December 31, 1899 is used as an arbitrary starting point. Therefore, January 1, 1900 is 1; January 2, 1900 is 2; and so on.

Exhibit: Examples of Date

367	January 1, 1901
31738	November 22, 1986

Time is represented as a decimal fraction of the 24-hour day. The number is between 0 and 1.

Exhibit: Examples of Time

.5	12:00:00 p.m.
.75	6:00:00 p.m.
.99999	11:59:59 p.m.
.083	2:00:00 a.m.

The two types of serial numbers when combined represent time and date together.

Example: 42815.14 represents 3:20 a.m. on 12 March, 2017.

Exhibit: Common Formats

m/d/yyyy	10/20/1994
d-mmm-yy	20-Oct-94
d-mmm	20-Oct (Current year assumed)
mmm-yy	Oct-94 (First day of the month assumed)
h:mm:ss AM/PM	03:25:00 a.m.
m/d/y h:mm	10/20/94 03:25

Exhibit: Codes Used for Custom Formats

Code	Comments
m	Displays the month as a number without leading zeros (1–12).
mm	Displays the month as a number with leading zeros (01–12).
mmm	Displays the month as an abbreviation (Jan–Dec).
mmmm	Displays the month as a full name (January–December).
mmmmm	Displays the first letter of the month (J–D).
d	Displays the day as a number without leading zeros (1–31).
dd	Displays the day as a number with leading zeros (01–31).
ddd	Displays the day as an abbreviation (Sun–Sat).
dddd	Displays the day as a full name (Sunday–Saturday).
yy or yyyy	Displays the year as a two-digit number (00–99) or as a four-digit number (1900–9999).
h or hh	Displays the hour as a number without leading zeros (0–23) or as a number with leading zeros (00–23).

m or mm	When used with a colon in a time format, displays the minute as a number without leading zeros (0–59) or as a number with leading zeros (00–59).
s or ss	Displays the second as a number without leading zeros (0–59) or as a number with leading zeros (00–59).
[]	Displays hours greater than 24 or minutes or seconds greater than 60.
AM/PM	Displays the hour using a 12-hour clock; if no AM/PM indicator is used, the hour uses a 24-hour clock.

*** **Pro Tip** ***
To display negative sign on the right: Home » Number Format » More Number Formats » Number » Custom   Then,   #,##0.00_-;#,##0.00-
To display text "Dollar" with numbers: Home » Number Format » More Number Formats » Number » Custom   #,##0.00 "(Dollar)"

Exhibit: Date-Related Functions

DATE	Returns the serial number of a particular date
DATEVALUE	Converts a date in the form of text to a serial number
DAY	Converts a serial number to a day of the month
DAYS	Returns the number of days between two dates
DAYS360	Calculates the number of days between two dates based on a 360-day year
EDATE	Returns the serial number of the date that represents the indicated number of months before or after the start date
EOMONTH	Returns the serial number of the last day of the month before or after a specified number of months
MONTH	Converts a serial number to a month
NETWORKDAYS	Returns the number of whole work days between two dates

NETWORKDAYS.INTL	An international version of the NETWORKDAYS function, which allows nonstandard weekend days
NOW	Returns the serial number of the current date and time
TODAY	Returns the serial number of today's date
WEEKDAY	Converts a serial number to a day of the week
WEEKNUM	Returns the week number in the year
WORKDAY	Returns the serial number of the date before or after a specified number of workdays
WORKDAY.INTL	An international version of the WORKDAY function, which allows nonstandard weekend days.
YEAR	Converts a serial number to a year
YEARFRAC	Returns the year fraction representing the number of whole days between start_date and end_date

B. DISPLAYING CURRENT DATE

TODAY function displays the current date in a cell.
NOW functions displays the date and time.

*** **Pro Tip** ***
Enter current date using Ctrl + ;   Enter current time using Ctrl + :

C. CONVERTING A NONDATE STRING TO A DATE

Example: Convert text string 20151026 into an actual date. (Assume text string is in A1).
=DATE (LEFT (A1,4), MID (A1,5,2), RIGHT (A1,2))

D. DETERMINING THE DATE OF THE MOST RECENT SUNDAY

=TODAY ()-MOD (TODAY ()-1,7)

E. SUMMING TIMES THAT EXCEED 24 HOURS

Example: Show the total time in B9.

	A	B	C
1	Day	Hours Spent	
2	Monday	0:56	
3	Tuesday	5:30	
4	Wednesday	8:15	
5	Thursday	10:14	
6	Friday	6:19	
7	Saturday	1:01	
8	Sunday	2:09	
9		=SUM (B2:B8)	

B8 will give the result "10:24".
To see the correct result,
Home » Number Format » More Number Formats » Custom
Then,
[h] : mm

F. CONVERTING FROM MILITARY TIME

(Assume military time is in A1)
=TIMEVALUE (LEFT (TEXT (A1, "0000"),2) & ":" & RIGHT (A1,2))
OR
=TIMEVALUE (TEXT (A1, "00\:00"))

6. TEXT FORMULAS

While Excel is used most commonly for crunching numbers, it can handle text very well too.

A. IDENTIFYING IF TWO STRINGS ARE IDENTICAL

=A1=A2
The formula returns TRUE or FALSE.
This method is not case sensitive.

= EXACT (A1, A2)
This method is case sensitive. The formula returns TRUE.

B. JOINING TWO OR MORE CELLS

There are two methods to do this. To join "Phil" and "Schiller", in A1 and A2, use:

a) A1&" "&A2
b) CONCATENATE (A1, " ", A2)

The " " is used to add a blank space between the two words.

C. CHANGING THE CASE OF TEXT

There are three functions:

1. UPPER converts the text to UPPERCASE.
2. LOWER converts the text to lowercase.
3. PROPER converts the text to Proper Case.

	A	B
1	hello world	=UPPER(A1)
2	Hello World	=LOWER(A2)
3	HELLO WORLD	=PROPER(A3)

Results in B1, B2 and B3 would be **HELLO WORLD**, **hello world**, and **Hello World**.

D. EXTRACTING CHARACTERS FROM A STRING

a) LEFT returns a specified number of characters from the beginning of a string.
b) RIGHT returns a specified number of characters from the end of a string.
c) MID returns a specified number of characters beginning at a specified position within a string.

E. REPLACING TEXT WITH OTHER TEXT

a) SUBSTITUTE replaces specific text in a string. Used when the character(s) to be replaced is known, but not the position.
b) REPLACE replaces text that occurs in a specific location within a string. Used when position of the text to be replaced is known, but not the actual text.

Example:
=SUBSTITUTE ("1954 Birthday", "1954", "1957")
The formula replaces 1954 with 1957 and returns 1957 Birthday.

=REPLACE ("Party/679",6,1, "")
The formula replaces the sixth character (/) and replaces with nothing.
The result is Party679.

F. FINDING AND SEARCHING WITHIN A STRING

FIND finds a substring within another text string and returns the starting position of the substring. The starting character position to begin searching can be specified.

SEARCH finds a substring within another text string and returns the starting position of the substring. The starting character position to begin searching can be specified.

*** Pro Tip ***

Use FIND for case-sensitive text comparisons. Wildcard comparisons are not supported.
Use SEARCH for non-case-sensitive text comparisons. Wildcard comparisons are supported.

Example:
=FIND ("H", "hello world How are You", 1)
The formula returns 13, the position of H in the string.

=SEARCH ("H", "hello world How are You", 1)
The formula returns 1, the first position of H (lowercase or uppercase) in the string.

G. COUNTING SPECIFIC CHARACTERS IN A CELL (UPPERCASE ONLY)

=LEN (A1)-LEN (SUBSTITUTE (A1, "B", ""))
The result reveals the number of Bs in the string.

H. COUNTING SPECIFIC CHARACTERS IN A CELL (UPPERCASE AND LOWERCASE)

=LEN (A1)-LEN (SUBSTITUTE (UPPER(A1), "B", ""))
The result reveals the number of Bs (uppercase and lowercase) in the string.

I. EXTRACTING THE FIRST WORD OF A STRING / EXTRACTING FIRST NAME

=LEFT (A1, FIND (" ", A1)-1)

J. EXTRACTING THE LAST WORD OF A STRING / EXTRACTING LAST NAME

=RIGHT (A1, LEN (A1)-FIND ("*", SUBSTITUTE (A1, " ", "*", LEN (A1)-LEN (SUBSTITUTE (A1, " ", "")))))

K. REMOVING TITLES FROM NAMES

=IF (OR (LEFT (A1,2) = "Mr", LEFT (A1,3) = "Mrs", LEFT(A1,2) = "Ms"), RIGHT (A1, LEN (A1)-FIND (" ", A1)), A1)

L. COUNTING THE NUMBER OF WORDS IN A CELL

=LEN (TRIM (A1))-LEN (SUBSTITUTE ((A1), " ", ""))+1

7. DATA VALIDATION

The Excel *data validation* feature you to set rules that define what can be entered into a cell.
Data » Data Tools » Data Validation

The following choices are available from the drop-down list:

a) **Any Value:** Removes existing data validation.
b) **Whole Number:** User must enter a whole number. Range can be specified.
c) **Decimal:** User must specify a number. Entry condition can be specified, such as greater than 5.
d) **List:** User must choose from a drop-down list provided.
e) **Date:** User must enter a date.
f) **Time:** User must enter a time.
g) **Text Length:** Length of the data is limited (measured in characters).
h) **Custom:** A logical formula determines the validity of the user's entry.

The Error message shown to the user can be customized.

*** Pro Tip ***

The Excel data validation feature suffers from a potentially serious problem: If the user copies a cell that does not use data validation and pastes it to a cell that does use data validation, the data validation rules are deleted. In other words, the cell then accepts any type of data. This has always been a problem, and Microsoft still has not fixed it in Excel 2016.

A. CREATING A DROP-DOWN LIST

To create a drop-down list:

a)   Enter the list items into a single-row or single-column range.
b)   Select the cell that will contain the drop-down list and then choose

Data » Data Tools » Data Validation

a)   From the Settings tab, select the List option (from the Allow drop-down list) and specify the range that contains the list, using the Source control. (The range can be in a different worksheet, but in the same workbook).
b)   In-Cell Dropdown check box is selected.

B. USING FORMULAS FOR DATA VALIDATION RULES

The power of data validation is utilized when data validation formulas are used. Specify a formula in the Data Validation dialog box by selecting the Custom option from the Allow drop-down list of the Settings tab. Enter the formula directly into the Formula control, or enter a reference to a cell that contains a formula. The Formula control appears on the Settings tab of the Data Validation dialog box when the Custom option is selected.

Examples are given.

a)   **Accepting text only** (Assume selected range is A1)
=ISTEXT (A1)

b)   **Accepting a larger value than the previous cell** (Assume active cell in selected range is A2)
=A1>A1

c)   **Accepting nonduplicate entries only**
The following formulas does not permit the user to make a duplicate entry in the range A1:C20.
=COUNTIF ($A$1:$C$20, A1) = 1

d)   **Accepting text that begins with a specific character** (Assume selected range is A1)
Text string beginning with letter Z (uppercase or lowercase) is allowed.
=LEFT(A1) = "a"

e)   **Accepting dates by the day of the week** (Assume selected range is A1)
The following formula ensures that the cell entry is a date, and is a Tuesday
=WEEKDAY(A1) = 3
The formula uses the WEEKDAY function, which returns 1 for Sunday, 2 for Monday, and so on.

8. PIVOT TABLES

Pivot table is a dynamic summary report that is generated from a database. The database can reside in a worksheet or an external data file. Pivot table helps transform rows and columns very quickly into a relevant representation.

Pivot tables are highly interactive, and allow for easy rearrangement of data. Reports can also be created easily by applying formatting.

*** Pro Tip ***
Unlike a formula-based summary report, a pivot table does not update automatically when information is changed in the source data. The Refresh needs to be done manually to update the Pivot table.

Example:

	A	B	C	D	E
1	State	Region	Month	Quarter	Sales
2	Delhi	North	Jan	Qtr-1	1,035
3	Delhi	North	Feb	Qtr-1	1,234
4	Delhi	North	Mar	Qtr-1	1,328
5	Rajasthan	North	Apr	Qtr-2	1,770
6	Rajasthan	North	May	Qtr-2	1,922
7	Rajasthan	North	Jun	Qtr-2	1,347
8	Mumbai	West	Jan	Qtr-1	1,581
9	Mumbai	West	Feb	Qtr-1	1,257
10	Mumbai	West	Mar	Qtr-1	1,343
11	Pune	West	Apr	Qtr-2	1,711
12	Pune	West	May	Qtr-2	1,999
13	Pune	West	Jun	Qtr-2	1,350
14	Kolkata	East	Jan	Qtr-1	1,719
15	Kolkata	East	Feb	Qtr-1	1,475
16	Kolkata	East	Mar	Qtr-1	1,951
17	Orissa	East	Apr	Qtr-2	1,689
18	Orissa	East	May	Qtr-2	1,441
19	Orissa	East	Jun	Qtr-2	1,427
20	Chennai	South	Jan	Qtr-1	1,361
21	Chennai	South	Feb	Qtr-1	1,163

22	Chennai	South	Mar	Qtr-1	1,072
23	Bengaluru	South	Apr	Qtr-2	1,110
24	Bengaluru	South	May	Qtr-2	1,099
25	Bengaluru	South	Jun	Qtr-2	1,423

To convert to a Pivot Table, Insert » Pivot Table

The PivotTable Field List on the right include the following:

a) Fields
b) Columns
c) Rows
d) Values

In case the pane is not visible, PivotTable Tools » Analyze » Field List

A. Pivot Table Terminology

	A	B	C	D
1	**Sum of Sales**	**Quarter**		
2	**Region**	**Qtr-1**	**Qtr-2**	**Grand Total**
3	**East**			
4	Kolkata	5145		5145
5	Orissa		4557	4557
6	**East Total**	**5145**	**4557**	**9702**
7	**North**			
8	Delhi	3597		3597
9	Rajasthan		5039	5039
10	**North Total**	**3597**	**5039**	**8636**
11	**South**			
12	Chennai	3596		3596
13	Bangalore		3632	3632
14	**South Total**	**3596**	**3632**	**7228**
15	**West**			
16	Mumbai	4181		4181
17	Pune		5060	5060

18	**West Total**	4181	5060	9241
19	**Grand Total**	16519	18288	34807

a) **Column labels:** This referes to a field that has a column orientation in the pivot table. A column is occupied by each item in the field. In the table, Quarter represents a column field containing two items (Qtr-1 and Qtr-2). There can be nested column fields.

b) **Grand totals:** This refers to a row or column that displays totals for all cells in a row or column in a pivot table. Grand totals can be calculated for rows, columns, or both (or neither). The pivot table in the figure shows grand totals for both rows and columns.

c) **Group:** This refers to a collection of items which are treated as a single item. These items can be grouped manually or automatically (group months into quarters, for example). The pivot table in the figure does not have any defined groups.

d) **Item:** This refers to an element in a field that appears as a row or column header in a pivot table. In the table, Qtr-1 and Qtr-2 are items for the Quarter field. The Region field has four items: East, North, South, West.

e) **Refresh:** This recalculates the pivot table after making changes to the source data.

f) **Row labels:** This refers to a field that has a row orientation in the pivot table. A row is occupied by each item in the field. There can be nested row fields.

g) **Source data:** This refers to the data that is used to create a pivot table. It can reside in a worksheet or an external database.

h) **Subtotals:** This refers to a row or column that displays subtotals for detail cells in a row or column in a pivot table. The pivot table in the figure displays subtotals for each region, below the data. Subtotals can be displayed above the data, or be hidden.

i) **Table Filter:** A field that has a page orientation in the pivot table. One item, multiple items, or all items in a page field at one time.

j) **Values area:** The cells in a pivot table that contain the summary data. Excel offers several ways to summarize the data (sum, average, count, and so on).

B. PIVOT TABLE CALCULATIONS

Pivot table data is most commonly summarized using the sum function. The Value Field Settings dialog box offers several techniques to summarize. The fastest way to display this dialog box is to right-click any value in the pivot table, and then choose Value Field Settings from the shortcut menu. This two tabs in this dialog box are: **Summarize Values By** and **Show Values As**.

The **Summarize Values By** tab allows selection of different summary functions. Options availabel are: Sum, Count, Average, Max, Min, Product, Count Numbers, StdDev, StdDevp, Var, and Varp.

To display values in a different form, select the drop-down control on the **Show Values As** tab. There are several options available, including as a percentage of the total or subtotal.

A number format can also be applied to the values using the dialog box.

C. CHANGING PIVOT TABLE ELEMENTS

PivotTable » Design » Layout
Various elements in the pivot table can be adjusted:

a) **Subtotals:** Hide subtotal, or choose where to display them (above or below the data).
b) **Grand Totals:** Choose which types, if any, to display.
c) **Report Layout:** Choose from three different layout styles (compact, outline, or tabular). Repeating labels can be hidden.
d) **Blank Row:** Add a blank row between items to improve readability.

*** Pro Tip ***
Copying a Pivot Table's content has limitations. • New columns or rows cannot be added • Calculated values cannot be changed • Formulas cannot be entered
The solution is to make a copy that is not linked to the data source. To do so, select the entire table and choose Home » Clipboard » Copy (or Ctrl + C). Then in a new worksheet, choose Home » Paste » Paste Values.
Please note that the copied information is *not* a pivot table, and is not linked to the source data.

D. CREATING A CALCULATED FIELD OR CALCULATED ITEM

Several users consider this as a highly confusing aspect. The features are very useful though, and are not complicated if the difference is understood.

a) **Calculated field:** This creates a new field from other fields in the pivot table. Assuming the pivot table source is a worksheet table, a substitute to using a calculated field is to add a new column to the table. This creates a formula to perform the required calculation. It should be noted that a calculated field must reside in the Values area of the pivot table. Calculated field cannot be used in the Columns area, in the Rows area, or in the Filter area.

PivotTable Tools » Analyze » Calculations » Fields, Items & Sets » Calculated Field (Any cell within the pivot table should be selected)

b) **Calculated item:** This uses the contents of other items within a field of the pivot table. Assuming the pivot table source is a worksheet table, a substitute to using a calculated item is to insert one or more rows and write formulas that use values in other rows. It should be noted that a calculated item must reside in the Columns area, Rows area, or Filters area of a pivot table. Calculated item cannot be used in the Values area.

PivotTable Tools » Analyze » Calculations » Fields, Items & Sets » Calculated Item (Cell pointer should be at Row Labels or Column Labels)

*** **Pro Tip** ***
Formulas used to create calculated fields and calculated items are not standard Excel formulas. The formulas are not entered in cells, but rather in dialog boxes.

E. SLICERS AND TIMELINE

Slicers are interactive tools that are an excellent substitutes to filter data present in a pivot table. The exact same type of filtering can be achieved by using the field labels in the pivot table. There are two key benefits of using slicers:

- It is intended for users who might not be comfortable using data filters.
- Attractive "dashboards" can be created.

PivotTable Tools » Analyze » Insert Slicer

Timeline is similar to Slicer, but designed specifically for time-based filtering. Timeline will only work when the field is formatted as a date, else will show an error.
PivotTable Tools » Analyze » Insert Timeline

F. REFERENCING CELLS WITHIN A PIVOT TABLE

When a formula refers to a cell within a pivot table, the cell references are replaced with the GETPIVOTDATA function. This ensures that the formula will continue to reference the intended cells if the pivot table layout is changed.

*** **Pro Tip** ***
The GETPIVOTDATA function is only used by Excel if the formula is created by pointing to the cell. If the cell reference is typed manually, Excel does not use the function.
GETPIVOTDATA function only works when the data is visible. If the table is modified and the value is not visible, the formula returns an error.

9. ARRAYS

An array is a collection of items. These items can be operated on together or individually. Excel has arrays that can be one dimensional or two dimensional. These dimensions correspond to rows and columns. For example, a one-dimensional array can be stored in a range that consists of one row (a horizontal array) or one column (a vertical array). A rectangular range of cells can store a two-dimensional array. Excel does not support three-dimensional arrays (the VBA programming language in Excel does support it).

A. A MULTICELL ARRAY FORMULA

Example: Calculate the result in the Total column

	A	B	C	D
1	**Product**	**Units Sold**	**Unit Price**	**Total**
2	BS-12	5	50	
3	BG-45	4	100	
4	MH-67	4	150	
5	DF-45	3	175	

The usual way would be to use = B2*C2 and then copy the formula down the column.

This would create 4 formulas in column D.

Using a multicell array formula, a single formula will be created which will return an array of 4 values.

To create an array formula:

a)   Select D2:D5
b)   Type the following formula
     =B2:B5*C2:C5
c)   Press Ctrl + Shift + Enter

*** Pro Tip ***

The contents of the cells that Excel entered will show a multiarray formula {=B2:B5*C2:C5}
Excel places curly brackets around the formula to indicate that it is an array formula.

This multicell array formula returns exactly the same values as these four normal formulas entered into individual cells in D2:D5:

=B2*C2
=B3*C3
=B4*C4
=B5*C5

There are various advantage to using a multicell array formula compared to individual formulas:

a) All formulas in a range are exactly the same.
b) The chances of a formula overwritten accidentally are reduced. One cell in a multicell array formula cannot be changed or deleted. If it is attempted, Excel displays an error message.
c) Novices are prevented from making accidental mistakes. Deliberate tampering of formulas can also be avoided.

There are also a few disadvantages:

a) It is impossible to insert a new row into the range.
b) If new data is added to the bottom of the range, modification needs to be done to the array formula so that the new data can be accommodated.

B. A SINGLE-CELL ARRAY FORMULA

Example: Calculate the sum of total product sales without individual calculations.

	A	B	C
1	**Product**	**Units Sold**	**Unit Price**
2	BS-12	5	50
3	BG-45	4	100
4	MH-67	4	150
5	DF-45	3	175
6			

The formula will be:
{=SUM (B2:B7*C2:C7)}

C. CREATING AN ARRAY CONSTANT

It is not necessary that an array is stored in a range of cells. It can be stored in memory also, in which case it is referred to as an *array constant*.

To create an array constant, the items need to be listed and surrounded with curly brackets.

Here is an example of a six-item horizontal array constant:
{1,0,1,0,1,0}

The following formula uses the SUM function, with the preceding array constant as its argument. The formula returns the sum of the values in the array (which is 3):
= SUM ({1,0,1,0,1,0})

*** Pro Tip ***

The formula uses an array, but the formula itself is not an array formula. Threfore, Ctrl + Shift + Enter is not used to enter the formula – although entering it as an array formula will still produce the same result.

Please note that we get the same result when we use:
= SUM ({1,0,1,0,1,0})

The advantage will become more clear with the following example.
This is an array formula that uses two array constants:
= SUM ({1,2,3,4} * {5,6,7,8})

The formula creates a new array (in memory) that consists of the product of the corresponding elements in the two arrays. The new array is
{5,12,21,32}

The SUM function then uses this new array as an argument. The result returned is (70). The formula is equivalent to the following formula, which does not use arrays:
= SUM (1*5, 2*6, 3*7, 4*8)

*** Pro Tip ***

Alternatively, the SUMPRODUCT function can also be used. The formula is not an array formula, but it uses two array constants as its arguments.
= SUMPRODUCT ({1,2,3,4}, {5,6,7,8})

Both an array constant and an array stored in a range can be used for a formula. The following formula, for example, returns the sum of the values in A1:C1, multiplying each by the corresponding element in the array constant:
= SUM ((A1:C1*{1,2,3,}))

This formula is equivalent to
= SUM (A1*1, B1*2, C1*3)

An array constant can contain logical values (TRUE or FALSE), text, numbers. It can also contain error values, such as #N/A. The number types can be in integer, decimal, or in a scientific format. Text must always be bounded in double quotation marks. The same array constant can use different types of values:

{1, 2, 3, TRUE, TRUE, FALSE, "Harry", "Ron", "Hermione"}

*** **Pro Tip** ***
An array constant cannot contain formulas, functions, or other arrays. Numeric values cannot contain dollar signs, commas, parentheses, or percent signs.

E. DIMENSIONS OF AN ARRAY

Arrays can be one dimensional or two dimensional. A one-dimensional array's orientation can be horizontal (corresponding to a single row) or vertical (corresponding to a single column).

One-dimensional horizontal arrays
Commas separate the elements in a one-dimensional horizontal array. The array can be displayed in a row of cells. An example of a one-dimensional horizontal array constant:

{1,2,3,4}

Four consecutive cells in a row are required to displaying this array in a range. To enter this array into a range, select a range of cells that consists of one row and four columns. Then enter

= {1,2,3,4,5} and press Ctrl + Shift + Enter.

*** **Pro Tip** ***
If an array is entered into a horizontal range that consists of more than four cells, the extra cells will contain #N/A (which denotes unavailable values). If the array is entered into a vertical range of cells, only the first item (1) will appear in each cell.

The following example is another horizontal array; it has seven elements and is made up of text strings:

{"Jan", "Feb", "Mar"}

To enter this array, select three cells in a row, type the following (and then press Ctrl + Shift + Enter):

= {"Jan", "Feb", "Mar"}

F. WORKING WITH ARRAY FORMULAS

Normal cell selection procedures can be used to manually select the cells that contain a multicell array formula. The following approaches can also be used:

a) Activate any cell in the array formula range. Choose Home » Editing » Find & Select » Go To, or just press F5. The Go To dialog box appears. In the Go To dialog box, click the Special button and then choose the Current Array option. Click OK to close the dialog box.

b) Press Ctrl+/ (forward slash) after activating any cell in the array formula range to select the cells that make up the array.

The entire range must be edited to edit an array formula that occupied multiple cells,.

*** Pro Tip ***

Rules to remember:

The contents of any individual cell that makes up an array formula cannot be changed.

Cells that make up part of an array formula cannot be moved (but an entire array formula can be moved).

Cells that form part of an array formula cannot be deleted (but an entire array can be deleted).

New cells cannot be inserted into an array range. Ths rule includes inserting rows or columns that would add new cells to an array range.

If a table was created by choosing Insert » Tables » Table, multicell array formulas cannot be used inside of that table. Similarly, if the range contains a multicell array formula, the range cannot be converted to a table.

G. EXPANDING OR CONTRACTING A MULTICELL ARRAY FORMULA

The following steps are to be performed:

a) Select the entire range that contains the array formula.
b) Press F2 to enter Edit mode.
c) Press Ctrl + Enter. Each selected cell now has an identical (non-array) formula
d) Additional or fewer cells can be selected. The active cell should be in a cell that is part of the original array.
e) Press F2 to re-enter Edit mode.
f) Press Ctrl + Shift + Enter.

H. EXAMPLES

a) Creating an array from values in a range

	A	B	C	D	E	F
1	2	Seal	1			
2	5	6	Dog			
3	3	TRUE	8			
4	panda	7	13			
5						
6				2	Seal	1
7				5	6	Dog
8				3	TRUE	8
9				panda	7	13
10						

The range D6:F9 contains a single array formula:
{= A1:C4}

The array in D8:F11 is linked to the range A1:C4. A change in any value in A1:C4 will result in a change in the corresponding cell in D8:F11. Values cannot be changed in D8:F11, as is a one-way link.

b) Performing operations on an array

The following array formula creates a rectangular array and multiplies each array element by 2:
{= {1,2,3,4;5,6,7,8;9,10,11,12} * 2}

c) Using functions with an array

Array can also perform worksheet functions. The following array formula, entered into a ten-cell vertical range, can be used to calculate the square root of each array element in the array constant:
{= SQRT ({1;2;3;4;5;6;7;8;9;10})}

If the range stores an array, a multicell array formula, the formula returns the square root of each value in the range:
{= SQRT (A1:A10)}

d) Transposing an array

Rows are converted to columns and columns to rows, when an array is transposed. A horizontal array can be converted to a vertical array (and vice versa). Use the TRANSPOSE function to transpose an array.

Take the example of the following one-dimensional horizontal array constant:
{1,2,3,4,5}

The TRANSPOSE function can be used to enter this array into a vertical range of cells. Five rows and one column need to be selected. Then enter the following formula and press Ctrl + Shift + Enter:
= TRANSPOSE ({1,2,3,4,5})

The horizontal array is transposed. The array elements appear in the vertical range.

e) Generating an array of consecutive integers

{= ROW (1:10)}
The formula generates a 21-element array that contains integers from 1 to 10.

f) Counting characters in a range

Example: Count length of characters in the cells. (Assume text string is in A1:A8).
{=SUM (LEN (A1:A8))}

g) Summing the three smallest values in a range

Example: Sum the 3 largest values in a range named Data.
{=SUM (SMALL (Data, {1, 2, 3}))}

h) Counting text cells in a range

Example: (Assume values are in A1:A5).
{=SUM (IF (ISTEXT (A1:A5), 1, 0))}
Or
{=SUM (ISTEXT (A1:A5) * 1)}

i) Counting the number of error values in a range

Example: Count errors in the range named Data.
{=SUM (IF (ISERROR (Data), 1, 0))}

Or
{=SUM (IF (ISERROR (Data) *1)}

j) Summing the n largest values in a range

Example: Add the 6 largest values in a range named Data.
{=SUM (LARGE (Data, ROW (INDIRECT ("1:6"))))}

k) Count the number of differences in two ranges

Example: (Assume two ranges are HisData and HerData).
{=SUM (IF (HisData = HerData, 0, 1))}
Or
{=SUM (1 * (HisData <> HerData))}

l) Determining whether a particular value appears in a range

Example: If the name exists, formula should display Found; else Not Found.
(Assume list of names as ListNames and name searched for as SearchName).
{=IF (OR (ListNames = SearchName, "Found", "Not Found")}

m) Returning the location of the maximum value in a range

Example: (Assume single column range named Data).
{=MIN (IF (Data = MAX (Data), ROW (Data), " "))}

n) Finding the row of a value's nth occurrence in a range

Example: (Assume single column range named Data and cell names Value).
{=SMALL (IF (Data = Value, ROW (Data), " "), n)}

The formula returns #NUM! if the Value is not found or if n exceeds the number of occurrences of Value in the range.

o) Returning the longest text in a range

Example: (Assume text string in a range named Data).
{=INDEX (Data, MATCH (MAX (LEN (Data)), LEN (Data), FALSE), 1)}

p) Summing every nth value in a range

Example: (Assume values are stored in a range named Data and value of *n* is in cell named *n*).

{=SUM (IF (MOD (ROW (INDIRECT ("1:" & COUNT (Data))) -1, n) = 0, Data, ""))}

q) Determining the closest value in a range

Example: (Assume values are stored in a range named Data and value being searched is Goal).
{=INDEX (Data, MATCH (SMALL (ABS (Target-Data), 1), ABS (Target - Data), 0))}

r) Returning the last value in a column

Example: (Assume values are in Column A and there are no empty cells).
{=OFFSET (A1, COUNTA (A:A) – 1, 0}

s) Returning the last value in a row

Example: (Assume values are in Row 1 and there are no empty cells).
{=INDEX (1:1, MAX (COLUMN (1:1) * (1:1 <> "")))}

The following are multicell array formulas and must be entered after selecting the range first and using Ctrl + Shift + Enter.

---

t) Returning only positive values from a range

Example: (Assume values are in single column vertical range named Data).
{=INDEX (Data, SMALL (IF (Data>0, ROW (INDIRECT ("1:" & ROWS (Data)))), ROW (INDIRECT ("1:" & ROWS (Data)))))}

u) Sorting a range of values dynamically

Example: (Assume values are in single column vertical range named Data).
{=LARGE (Data, ROW (INDIRECT ("1:" & ROWS (Data))))}

v) Returning a list of unique items in a range

Example: (Assume values are in single column vertical range named Data).
{=INDEX (Data, SMALL (IF (MATCH (Data, Data, 0) = ROW (INDIRECT ("1:" & ROWS (Data))), MATCH (Data, Data, 0), ""), ROW (INDIRECT ("1:" & ROWS (Data)))))}

10. WHAT-IF ANALYSIS AND GOAL SEEK

Excel can create dynamic models, which uses formulas that instantly recalculate when values are changed in cells used by formulas. A *what-if* analysis refers to changing cell values in a systematic manner, and observing effects on specific formula cells.

A. TYPES OF WHAT-IF

The three basic options are:

a) **Manual what-if analysis:** Plug in new values and observe the effects on formula cells.
b) **Data tables:** Create a table that displays the results of selected formula cells, as one or two input cells are systematically changed.
c) **Scenario Manager:** Create scenarios with names; generate reports that use outlines or pivot tables.

B. CREATING A ONE-INPUT DATA TABLE

This displays the results of one or more formulas for various values of a single input cell. The table needs to be set up manually. The table can be placed anywhere in the worksheet. The left column contains various values for the single input cell. The top row contains references to formulas located elsewhere in the worksheet. A single formula reference or any number of formula references can be used. The upper-left cell of the table remains empty. Excel calculates the values that result from each value of the input cell, which are then placed under each formula reference.

Example: Create a one-input data table.

	A	B	C	D	E	F	G	H	I
1									
2						*Loan Amt*	*Mo Pmt*	*Total Pmts*	*Total Int*
3		**Input Cells**				**$3,79,061**	**$2,450**	**$5,87,900**	**$2,08,839**
4		Purchase Price:	$4,12,023		**5.00%**				
5		Down Payment:	8%		**5.25%**				
6		Loan Term:	240		**5.50%**				

7	Interest Rate (Months):	4.75%	5.75%				
8			6.00%				
9	**Result Cells**		6.25%				
10	Loan Amount:	$3,79,061	6.50%				
11	Monthly Payment:	$2,450	6.75%				
12	Total Payments:	$5,87,900	7.00%				
13	Total Interest:	$2,08,839					

The formulas have the following formulas / function / reference:

CELL C10 FORMULA:	=C4*(1-C5)
CELL C11 FUNCTION:	=PMT(C7/12, C6,-C10)
CELL C12 FORMULA:	=C11*C6
CELL C13 FORMULA:	=C12-C10
CELL F3 FORMULA:	=C10
CELL G3 FORMULA:	=C11
CELL H3 FORMULA:	=C12
CELL I3 FORMULA:	=C13

To create the data table, select the data table range (E3:I12) and choose
Data » Data Tools » What-If Analysis » Data Table
Enter $C$7 in the Column Input Cell field.

The cells will be filled with calculated results.

	A	B	C	D	E	F	G	H	I
1									
2							*Mo*		
						Loan Amt	*Pmt*	*Total Pmts*	*Total Int*
3		**Input Cells**				$3,79,061	$2,450	$5,87,900	$2,08,839
4		Purchase Price:	$4,12,023		5.00%	$3,79,061	$2,398	$5,75,551	$1,96,490

5		Down Payment:	8%		5.25%	$3,79,061	$2,450	$5,87,900	$2,08,839
6		Loan Term:	240		5.50%	$3,79,061	$2,502	$6,00,393	$2,21,331
7		Interest Rate (Months):	4.75%		5.75%	$3,79,061	$2,554	$6,13,028	$2,33,966
8					6.00%	$3,79,061	$2,608	$6,25,803	$2,46,742
9		**Result Cells**			6.25%	$3,79,061	$2,661	$6,38,718	$2,59,657
10		Loan Amount:	$3,79,061		6.50%	$3,79,061	$2,716	$6,51,771	$2,72,710
11		Monthly Payment:	$2,450		6.75%	$3,79,061	$2,771	$6,64,960	$2,85,898
12		Total Payments:	$5,87,900		7.00%	$3,79,061	$2,826	$6,78,283	$2,99,222
13		Total Interest:	$2,08,839			$3,79,061	$2,398	$5,75,551	$1,96,490

*** Pro Tip ***

The contents of the cells that Excel entered will show a multiarray formula
{=TABLE (,C7)}
An array formula is a single formula that can produce results in multiple cells.
Since the table uses formulas, Excel updates the table if the cell references
are changed in the first row or different interest rates are plugged in the first
column.

C. CREATING A TWO-INPUT DATA TABLE

This allows two input cells to be varied. The key difference is that it can show
the results of only one formula at a time. Any number of formulas or references to
formulas can be placed across the top row of the table in a one-input table. In a two-
input table, this top row holds the values for the second input cell. The upper-left cell
of the table contains a reference to the single result formula.

D. SCENARIO MANAGER

Data tables have the following limitations:

a) Variation can only be done to one or two input cells at a time.
b) It is not easy to set up a data table.
c) Two-input data table shows the results of only one formula cell.

Few select combinations can be seen in Scenario manager. This is used when all possible combinations are not required. Different sets of input values (called *changing cells*) for any number of variables are to be stored. A name can be given to each set. Excel displays the worksheet by using the values, when a set of values are selected. A summary report can also be generated, which shows the effect of various combinations of values on any number of result cells.

Example: Create a scenario model that shows the following possible scenarios:

Scenario	Hourly Cost	Materials Cost
Best Case	40	60
Worst Case	50	70
Most Likely	45	65

	A	B	C	D	E
1	**Resource Cost Variables**				
2	Hourly Labour Cost	40			
3	Material Cost	60			
4					
5					
6		**Product A**	**Product B**	**Product C**	
7	Hours per unit	12	14	24	
8	Material per unit	6	9	14	
9	Cost to produce	$840	$1,100	$1,800	
10	Sales price	$795	$1,295	$2,195	
11	Unit profit	-$45	$195	$395	
12	Units produced	36	18	12	
13	**Total profit per product**	-$1,620	$3,510	$4,740	
14					
15	**Total Profit**	$6,630			

Choose Data » Data Tools » What-If Analysis » Data Table
Click the Add button in the dialog box.
Write "Best Case" in Scenario name, and "B2:B3" in Changing cells.

TERMINOLOGY

a) **Scenario Name:** You can give the scenario any name that you like – preferably something meaningful.

b) **Changing Cells:** The input cells for the scenario. The cell addresses can be selected directly or selected by pointing.

c) Nonadjacent cells are allowed; if pointing to multiple cells, press Ctrl while clicking the cells. Each named scenario can use the same set of changing cells or different changing cells. The number of changing cells for a scenario is limited to 32.

d) **Comment:** By default, Excel displays the name of the person who created the scenario and the date when it was created. This text can be changed, new text added to it, or deleted.

e) **Protection:** The two protection options (preventing changes and hiding a scenario) are in effect only when the worksheet is protected and Scenario option in the Protect Sheet dialog box is chosen. Protecting a scenario prevents anyone from modifying it; a hidden scenario does not appear in the Scenario Manager dialog box.

Displaying and Editing Scenarios:

Data » Data Tools » What-If Analysis » Scenario Manager
Select the Scenario to be displayed and click on Show.
To edit click the Edit button.

Generating a Scenario Report:

Scenario summary report documents all the multiple scenarios.
Data » Data Tools » What-If Analysis » Scenario Manager
Select the Summary button.
There are two choices:

a) Scenario Summary: The summary report appears in the form of a worksheet outline.

b) Scenario PivotTable: The summary report appears in the form of a pivot table.

E. GOAL SEEK

This determines the value needed to be entered in a single output cell to produce a result we want in a dependent (formula) cell.

Example: Change the value in C4 so that the value in C11 becomes $5,000.

	A	B	C
1			
2			
3		**Input Cells**	
4		Purchase Price:	$5,00,000
5		Down Payment:	15%
6		Loan Term (Months):	180
7		Interest Rate (APR):	8.50%
8			
9		**Result Cells**	
10		Loan Amount:	$4,25,000
11		Monthly Payment:	$4,185
12		Total Payments:	$7,53,326
13		Total Interest:	$3,28,326
14			

Choose Data » Data Tools » What-If Analysis » Goal Seek

In the dialog box, put $C$11 in Set Cell, 5000 in To value, and $C$4 in By changing cell.

Click OK to replace the original value, or click Cancel to restore your worksheet to the original value.

*** Pro Tip ***

Adjust the maximum iterations setting on the Formulas tab of Excel Options dialog box. (File » Options)

---

11. STATISTICAL FUNCTIONS

The Analysis ToolPak extends analytical ability to Excel.

*** Pro Tip ***

Since the Analysis ToolPak is an add-in, it needs to be installed.

If you cannot access Data » Analysis » Data Analysis, install the add-in.

Choose File » Options, select Add-Ins tab, select Excel Add-Ins from drop-down list, click Go, place a check mark next to Analysis ToolPak.

A. Using the Analysis Tools

Choose Data » Analysis » Data Analysis and select the analysis tool. Usually one or more Input ranges needs to be specified, plus an Output range (one cell is sufficient). Alternatively, the results can be placed on a new worksheet or in a new workbook. The procedures vary in the amount of additional information required. In several dialog boxes, it can be specified if the Data range includes labels. By specifying the entire range, including the labels, and indicating to Excel that the first column (or row) contains labels, Excel will use these labels in the tables that it produces. Most tools also provide different output options that can be selected, based on requirements.

*** Pro Tip ***

The Analysis ToolPak output is inconsistent. In some cases, the procedures use formulas, and the data can be changed, and results update automatically. In some procedures, the results are stored as values, and results are unchanged when data is changed.

Analysis ToolPak Tools

There are various tools available, listed below (but not limited to):

a) Analysis of Variance

Analysis of Variance (sometimes abbreviated as *Anova*) is a statistical test that determines whether two or more samples were drawn from the same population. Using tools in the Analysis ToolPak, three types of analysis of variance can be performed:

- Single-factor: A one-way analysis of variance, with only one sample for each group of data.
- Two-factor with replication: A two-way analysis of variance, with multiple samples (or replications) for each group of data.
- Two-factor without replication: A two-way analysis of variance, with a single sample (or replication) for each group of data.

The output for this test consists of the means and variances for each of the samples, the value of F, the critical value of F, and the significance of F (P-value).

b) Correlation

Correlation measures the degree to which two sets of values vary together. For example, if lower values in one data set are typically associated with lower values in the second data set, the two data sets have a positive correlation. The degree of correlation is expressed as a coefficient that ranges from −1.0 (a perfect negative correlation) to +1.0 (a perfect positive correlation). A correlation coefficient of 0 indicates that the two variables are not correlated.

The output consists of a correlation matrix that shows the correlation coefficient for each variable paired with every other variable.

*** **Pro Tip** ***
The resulting correlation matrix does not use formulas to calculate the results. Therefore, if any data changes, the correlation matrix is not valid. If the CORREL function is used, the correlation matrix changes automatically when data is changed.

c) Covariance

The Covariance tool produces a matrix that is similar to the one generated by the Correlation tool. Covariance, like correlation, measures the degree to which two variables vary together. Specifically, covariance is the average of the product of the deviations of each data point pair from their respective means.

*** **Pro Tip** ***
The Covariance tool does not generate formulas. COVAR function is an alternative.

d) Descriptive Statistics

Descriptive statistics produces a table with standard statistics. The procedure consists of values, and not formulas. This procedure can only be used when the data is not going to change.

e) Exponential Smoothing

Exponential Smoothing is a technique for predicting data that is based on the previous data point and the previously predicted data point. The damping factor (also known as a smoothing constant) can be specified, which can range from 0 to 1. This factor determines the relative weighting of the previous data point and the previously predicted data point. Standard errors and a chart can also be displayed.

The exponential smoothing procedure generates formulas that use the damping factor that is specified. Excel updates the formulas if the data changes.

f) F-test (two sample test for variance)

An F-test is a commonly used statistical test that enables comparison of two population variances.

The output for this test consists of the means and variances for each of the two samples, the value of F, the critical value of F, and the significance of F.

g) Moving Average

The Moving Average tool helps smooth out a data series that has a lot of variability.

This procedure is often used in conjunction with a chart. Excel does the smoothing by computing a moving average of a specified number of values.

The number of values that Excel uses for each average can be specified. If the Standard Errors check box in the Moving Average dialog box is selected, Excel calculates standard errors and places formulas for these calculations next to the moving average formulas.

The standard error values indicate the degree of variability between the actual values and the calculated moving averages.

h) Regression

Regression analysis enables us to determine the extent to which one range of data (the dependent variable) varies as a function of the values of one or more other ranges of data (the independent variables). This relationship is expressed mathematically, using values that Excel calculates. These calculations can be used to create a mathematical model of the data and predict the dependent variable by using different values of one or more independent variables. This tool can perform simple and multiple linear regressions and calculate and standardize residuals automatically.

The Regression dialog box offers many options:

- Input Y Range: The range that contains the dependent variable.
- Input X Range: One or more ranges that contain independent variables.
- Confidence Level: The confidence level for the regression.
- Constant Is Zero: If selected, forces the regression to have a constant of 0 (which means that the regression line passes through the origin; when the X values are 0, the predicted Y value is 0).
- Residuals: The four options in this section of the dialog box enable specifying whether to include residuals in the output. Residuals are the differences between observed and predicted values.
- Normal Probability: Generates a chart for normal probability plots.

i) T-Test

The T-Test tool determines whether a statistically significant difference exists between two small samples. Three types of t-tests can be performed by Analysis ToolPak:

- Paired two-sample for means: For paired samples in which there are two observations on each subject (such as a pretest and a post-test). The samples must be the same size.
- Two-sample assuming equal variances: For independent, rather than paired, samples. Excel assumes equal variances for the two samples.
- Two-sample assuming unequal variances: For independent, rather than paired, samples. Excel assumes unequal variances for the two samples.

B. LIST OF STATISTICAL FUNCTIONS

The following exhibit lists statistical functions that have some utility in the business world.

Exhibit: Statistical functions

Function	Description
=AVEDEV	Returns the average of the absolute deviations of the numeric arguments from their mean value.
=AVERAGE	Returns the average of the numeric arguments.
=AVERAGEA	Returns the average of the arguments, which can be non-numeric.
=AVERAGEIF	Returns the average for those cells in range that satisfy the criteria.
=AVERAGEIFS	Returns the average for those cells in multiple ranges that satisfy their corresponding criteria.
=CORREL	Returns the correlation coefficient.
=COUNT	Counts the numbers in the argument list.
=COUNTA	Counts the values (numeric and non-numeric) in the argument list.
=COUNTBLANK	Counts the empty cells in range.
=COUNTIF	Returns the count of those cells in range that satisfy the criteria.
=COUNTIFS	Returns the count of those cells in multiple ranges that satisfy their corresponding criteria.
=COVARIANCE.P	Returns the population covariance, which is the average of the products of deviations for each data point pair.
=F.TEST	Returns an F-test result, the one-tailed probability that the variances in the two sets are not significantly different.

=FORECAST. LINEAR	Returns a forecast value for x based on a linear regression of the arrays known_y's and known_x's.
=FREQUENCY	Returns a frequency distribution.
=GROWTH	Returns values along an exponential trend.
=INTERCEPT	Returns the y-intercept of the linear regression trend line generated by the known_y's and known_x's.
=KURT	Returns the kurtosis of a frequency distribution.
=LARGE	Returns the kth largest value in array.
=LINEST	Uses the least squares method to calculate a straight-line regression fit through the known_y's and known_x's.
=LOGEST	Uses the least squares method to calculate an exponential regression fit through the known_y's and known_x's.
=MAX	Returns the maximum value.
=MAXA	Returns the maximum value, including text and Boolean values.
=MEDIAN	Returns the median value.
=MIN	Returns the minimum value.
=MINA	Returns the minimum value, including text and Boolean values.
=MODE.MULTI	Returns an array of the most common values.
=MODE.SNGL	Returns the most common value.
=NORM.DIST	Generates the normal distribution by returning the probability that x exists within a population.
=PERCENTILE.EXC	Returns the kth percentile of the values in array, where k is between 0 and 1, exclusive.
=PERCENTILE.INC	Returns the kth percentile of the values in array, where k is between 0 and 1, inclusive.
=PERMUT	Returns the total possible permutations, given number items and number_chosen items in each permutation.
=RANK.AVG	Returns the rank of a number in a list or the average rank if more than one value has the same rank.
=RANK.EQ	Returns the rank of a number in a list or the first rank if more than one value has the same rank.
=RSQ	Returns the rank of determination that indicates how much of the variance in the known_y's is is due to the known_x's.
=SKEW	Returns the skewness of a frequency distribution.

=SLOPE	Returns the slope of the linear regression trend generated by the known_y's and known_x's.
=SMALL	Returns the kth smallest value in array.
=STDEV.P	Returns the standard deviation based on an entire population.
=STDEV.S	Returns the standard deviation based on a sample.
=STDEVA	Returns the standard deviation based on a sample, which can include non-numeric values.
=STDEVPA	Returns the standard deviation based on an entire population, which can include non-numeric values.
=T.TEST	Returns the probability associated with a t-test.
=TREND	Returns values along a linear trend.
=VAR.P	Returns the variance based on an entire population.
=VAR.S	Returns the variance based on a sample.
=VARA	Returns the variance based on a sample, which can include non-numeric values.
=VARPA	Returns the variance based on an entire population, which can include non-numeric values.
=Z.TEST	Returns the p-value of a two-sample z-test for means with known variances.

12. FINANCIAL APPLICATIONS

The *time value* of money is a concept involving calculating the value of money in the past, present, or future. The premise is that money increases value over time because of interest earned by the money. Money invested today will be worth more tomorrow.

A. KEY CONCEPTS

a) **Present value:** This is the principal amount. $10,000 deposited in a bank savings account represents the principal, or present value, of the money invested. If $20,000 is borrowed to purchase a car, this amount represents the principal, or present value, of the loan. Present value may be positive or negative.

b) **Future value (FV):** This is the principal plus interest. If $1,000 for five years and earn 3% annual interest, the investment is worth $5,796.37 at the end of the five-year term. This amount is the future value of the $5,000 investment. If a three-year car loan for $15,000 is taken, and monthly payments made based on a 5.25% annual interest rate, a total of $16,244.97 is paid. This amount represents the principal plus the interest you paid. Future value may be positive or negative, depending on the perspective (lender or borrower).

c) **Payment (PMT):** This is either principal or principal plus interest. If $100 deposited per month into a savings account, $100 is the payment. If there is a monthly mortgage payment of $1,025, this amount is made up of principal and interest.

d) **Interest rate:** Interest is a percentage of the principal, usually expressed on an annual basis. For example, 2.5% annual interest may be earned on a bank CD (certificate of deposit).

e) **Period:** This represents the point in time when interest is paid or earned (for example, a bank CD that pays interest quarterly, or an auto loan that requires monthly payments).

f) **Term:** This is the amount of time of interest. A 12-month bank CD has a term of one year. A 20-year mortgage loan has a term of 240 months.

Exhibit: Argument Descriptions

Function Argument	Description
Rate	The interest rate per period. If the rate is expressed as an annual interest rate, it must be divided by the number of periods.
Nper	The total number of payment periods.
Per	A particular period. The period must be less than or equal to nper.
Pmt	The payment made each period (a constant value that does not change).
Fv	The future value after the last payment is made. If it is omitted, it is assumed to be 0. (The future value of a loan, for example, is 0.)
Type	Indicates when payments are due – either 0 (due at the end of the period) or 1 (due at the beginning of the period). If it is omitted, it is assumed to be 0.
Guess	Used by the RATE function. An initial estimate of what the result will be. The RATE function is calculated by iteration. If the function does not converge on a result, changing the guess argument will help.

B. WORKSHEET FUNCTIONS FOR CALCULATING LOAN INFORMATION

a) PMT

The PMT function returns the loan payment (principal plus interest) per period, assuming constant payment amounts and a fixed interest rate. The syntax for the PMT function is

PMT (rate, nper, pv, fv, type)

The following formula returns the monthly payment amount for a $8,000 loan with a 5% annual percentage rate. The loan has a term of three years (36 months).

=PMT (5%/12, 36, -8000)

b) PPMT

The PPMT function returns the principal part of a loan payment for a given period, assuming constant payment amounts and a fixed interest rate. The syntax for the PPMT function is

PPMT (rate, per, nper, pv, fv, type)

The following formula returns the amount paid to principal for a $8,000 loan with a 5% annual percentage rate. The loan has a term of three years (36 months).

=PPMT (5%/12, 1, 36, -8000) [can also use cells]

*** **Pro Tip** ***
Use CUMPRINC to calculate the cumulative principal paid between any two payment periods.

c) IPMT

The IPMT function returns the interest part of a loan payment for a given period, assuming constant payment amounts and a fixed interest rate. The syntax for the IPMT function is

IPMT (rate, per, nper, pv, fv, type)

The following formula returns the amount paid to interest for the first month of a $8,000 loan with a 5% annual percentage rate. The loan has a term of three years (36 months).

=IPMT (5%/12, 1, 36, -8000)

*** **Pro Tip** ***
Use CUMIPMT to calculate the cumulative interest paid between any two payment periods.

d) RATE

The RATE function returns the periodic interest rate of a loan, given the number of payment periods, the periodic payment amount, and the loan amount. The syntax for the RATE function is
RATE (nper, pmt, pv, fv, type, guess)

The following formula calculates the annual interest rate for a 36-month loan for $8,000 that has a monthly payment amount of $121.83.
=RATE (48, 121.83, -8000) * 12

e) NPER

The RATE function returns the number of payment periods for a loan, given the loan's amount, interest rate, and periodic payment amount. The syntax for the NPER function is
NPER (rate, pmt, pv, fv, type)

The following formula calculates the number of payment periods for a $8,000 loan that has a monthly payment amount of $121.83. The loan has a 5% annual interest rate.
=NPER (5%/12, 121.83, -8000)

f) PV

The PV function returns the present value i.e. the original loan amount for a loan, given the interest rate, the number of periods, and the periodic payment amount. The syntax for the PV function is
PV (rate, nper, pmt, fv, type)

The following formula calculates the original loan amount for a 36-month loan that has a monthly payment amount of $121.83. The loan has a 5% annual interest rate.
=PV (5%/12, 36, 121.83, -8000)

13. CONCLUSION

With increasing amounts of data being generated, and consequently being available for analysis, there are new applications emerging. The role of Excel has remained steadfast though. It continues to remain the de facto spreadsheet program used by everyone ranging from students to CXOs. Its versatility continues to improve with more and more Add-Ins available which increase the functionality of the software. Additionally, use of VB and Macros open up infinite possibilities for Excel, such as preparing dashboards, automation of tasks, customized solutions etc. While intermediate users can benefit from the available options, advanced users should explore Excel's robust programming capabilities as well.

14. SHORTCUTS

Exhibit: Navigating Worksheets

Arrow keys	Navigate by one cell at a time in any direction
Page Down / Page Up	Move one screen down / up
Alt + Page Down / Page Up	Move one screen right / left
Tab / Shift + Tab	Move one cell to the right / to the left in a worksheet
Ctrl + Arrow Keys	Move to the edge of next data region (cells that contain data)
Home	Move to the beginning of row
Ctrl + Home	Move to the beginning of worksheet
Ctrl + End	Move to the last cell with content of worksheet.
Ctrl + G	Display the Go To dialog box
Ctrl + G then type e.g. A50	Go to line 50, Column A

Exhibit: Cell Selection (Basic)

Shift + Arrow Keys	Extend selection by one cell
Shift + Page Down / Page Up	Extend selection screen down / up
Ctrl + Shift + Arrow Keys	Extend selection to next non-blank cell
Shift + Home	Extend selection to beginning of the row
Ctrl + A with no data nearby current cell	Select all
Ctrl + A with data nearby current cell	Select all cells in data-containing area. Press twice to select everything.
Ctrl + Shift + Home	Extend selection to first cell of the worksheet
Ctrl + Shift + End	Extend selection to last used cell on the worksheet (lower-right corner)
Shift + F8	Lock Selection Extend Mode

Exhibit: Cell Selection (Column and Row Selection)

Shift + Space	Select current row
Shift + Space, then Shift + Arrow Down / Arrow Up	Select current row, then expand selection by one row down / up
Shift + Space, then Shift + Page Down / Page Up	Select current row, then expand selection by one page down / up
Ctrl + Space	Select current column
Ctrl + Space, then Shift + Arrow Right / Arrow Left	Select current column, then expand selection by one column right / left
Ctrl + Space, then Shift + Alt + Page Down / Page Up	Select current column. then expand selection by one screen right / left

Exhibit: Juggle Rows, Columns and Cells

Shift + Space, then Ctrl + -	Select single row; then delete
Shift + Space, Shift + Arrow Up / Arrow Down, then Ctrl + -	Select multiple rows: then delete
Shift + Space, Ctrl + Shift + +	Select single row; then insert one row above
Shift + Space, Shift + Arrow Up / Arrow Down, then Ctrl + +	Select multiple rows; then insert the same number rows below
Ctrl + Space, then Ctrl + -	Select single (or multiple) columns, then delete
Ctrl + Space, then Ctrl + Shift + +	Select single row, then insert row below. Select multiple to insert multiple rows
Ctrl + Shift + + with row(s) in clipboard and a row selected	Paste Insert - paste row(s) from clipboard and shift existing content downward
Ctrl + Shift + + with column(s) in clipboard and a column selected	Paste Insert - paste column(s) from clipboard and shift existing content to the right
Ctrl + Shift + +	With cells that are not complete rows / columns - Open insert cell / column menu

Ctrl + -	With cells that are not complete rows / columns - Open delete cell / row / column menu
Shift + Arrow Down, F2, then Ctrl + Enter	Fill single cell content down to all cells selected with Shift + Arrow Down
Shift + Arrow Up, F2, then Ctrl + Enter	Fill single cell content up to all cells selected with Shift + Arrow Down

Exhibit: Edit Cell Content

F2	Edit cell. Press Esc to cancel
Home / End	Jump to beginning / end of cell
Arrow Keys	Navigate by one character left / right or one line up / down
Ctrl + Arrow Left / Arrow Right	Navigate by one word left / right
Shift + Arrow Keys	Select one character to the left/ right (or one line up /down)
Shift + Home / End	Select from the insertion point to beginning / end of cell
Ctrl + Shift + Arrow Left / Arrow Right	Select or unselect one word to the left / right
Delete / Backspace	Delete one character to the right / left of cursor
Ctrl + Delete	Delete from cursor to end of cell
Alt + Enter	Start a new line inside cell
Enter / Shift + Enter	Complete cell entry and move one cell down / up
Tab / Shift + Tab	Complete cell entry and move one cell right / left
Ctrl + Enter	Complete cell entry and do not move selection
Ctrl +'	Duplicate value from cell above into current cell at cursor position
Ctrl + ;	Insert current date at cursor position
Ctrl + Shift + ;	Insert current time at cursor position

Exhibit: Duplicate Cells, Rows and Columns

| Ctrl + D | Fill Down from cell(s) above into current cell(s) |
| Ctrl + D with a row selected | Duplicate row via fill down - Fill current row with content from row above |

Ctrl + D with multiple empty cells selected	Duplicate content of first cell(s) in first row to all cells in selection downward
Ctrl + R	Fill Right from cell(s) on the left into current cell(s)
Ctrl + R with a column selected	Duplicate column via fill right - Fill current column with content from column on the left
Ctrl + D with multiple empty cells selected	Duplicate content first cell(s) in first column to all cells in selection to the right
Ctrl +'	Duplicate formula from cell above

Exhibit: Undo, Redo and Repeat Action

Ctrl + Z	Undo
Ctrl + Y	Redo (after undo) or Repeat (e.g. when applying formats)
Alt + 2	Undo list (via quick access). Use Arrow Down to extend undo range.
Alt + 3	Redo list (via quick access). Use Arrow Down to extend redo range.
Alt + Enter	Repeat last action

Exhibit: Cut, Copy, Paste and Paste Special

Ctrl + X	Cut cell(s) to clipboard
Ctrl + C	Copy cell(s) to clipboard
Ctrl + V	Paste cell(s) from clipboard
Ctrl + +	Insert Paste - Paste cell and push content downward or rightward. Works great for entire rows and columns.
Ctrl + Alt + V	Open paste Special Menu (requires a prior copy to Clipboard)
Ctrl + Alt + V, then V, Enter	Paste Values
Ctrl + Alt + V, then T, Enter	Paste Formats
Ctrl + Alt + V, then E, Enter	Paste Transposed
Ctrl + Alt + V, then W, Enter	Paste Column Width
Ctrl + Alt + V, then U, Enter	Paste Values and Number Formats
F3	Paste a defined name into a formula

Exhibit: Format Cells - General Cell Format

Ctrl + Alt + V, then T and Enter	Copy a cell via Ctrl + C, then via Paste Special, paste format of that cell to current cell
Alt + Enter	Repeat a previous cell format action on current cell
Ctrl + 1	Open Format Cells dialog with last selection active
Ctrl + Shift + F	Open Format Cells dialog with Font Tab active

Exhibit: Format Cells – Font Face, Font Decoration and Cell Color

Ctrl + B	Apply / remove bold format
Ctrl + I	Apply / remove italic format
Ctrl + U	Apply / remove underline format
Ctrl + 5	Apply / remove strikethrough formatting
Alt + H, FF	Home select Font Face; type font name supported by auto-complete, or use to Arrow Down to select
Alt + H, FS	Home select Font Size: use Arrow Key, then Enter to change size
Alt + H, FC, Escape, Enter	Assign current font colour to selection via Home Font Color. While escaping the font-colour drop-down, the focus stays on the icon; press Enter to assign the current colour
Alt + HH, Escape, Enter	Assign current fill colour to selection fill colour via Home Highlight Cell. While escaping the font-colour drop-down, the focus stays on the icon; press Enter to assign the current colour
Alt + HH, then N	Set to No fill colour

Exhibit: Format Cells – Number Formats

Ctrl + Shift + ~	Apply the general number format (e.g. 1000)
Ctrl + Shift + 1	Apply the number format with two decimal places, thousands separator (e.g. 1,000.00)
Ctrl + Shift + 2	Apply the time format with the hour and minute, and indicate AM or PM
Ctrl + Shift + 3	Apply the date format with the day, month, and year

Ctrl + Shift + 4	Apply the currency format with two decimal places (e.g. $1,000.00)
Ctrl + Shift + 5	Apply the percentage format with no decimal places (e.g. 10%)
Ctrl + Shift + 6	Apply the scientific number format

Exhibit: Find and Replace

Ctrl + F	Display the Find and Replace dialog box (with find selected)
Ctrl + H	Display the find and replace dialog box (with replace selected)
Escape	Close the find and replace dialog Box (with focus on dialog box)
Shift + F4	Find next (with search box closed)
Ctrl + Shift + F4	Find previous (with search box closed)
Alt + Tab, or Ctrl + F / H when losing focus	Toggle focus between find / replace dialog box and worksheet
Alt + F	Find next with find dialog box active
Alt + I	Find all with find dialog box active
* In search option	Use as asterix for searching multiple characters
? in search options	Use as wildcard for searching any single character, use '~' before '?' when searching special characters ~* searches for * ~~ searches for ~ ~? searches for?

Exhibit: Formulas - Basics

=	Start a formula
Alt + =	Insert the AutoSum formula
Ctrl + A with formula present	Edit formula in formula bar
Ctrl + Shift + U	Expand / collapse formula bar
F4	After typing cell reference makes reference absolute. Repeat if you want to toggle from absolute reference to partial or complete removal.
Shift + F3 with empty cell	Display the insert function; dialog box

Shift + F3 with formula present	Edit arguments of formula at cursor position
Alt + H, FD, U	Select all Formulas (Home – Find – Formulas)
Ctrl + Shift + Enter with array formula	Enter a formula as an array formula. Editing will require Ctrl + Shift + Enter.
Ctrl + ~	Show / hide all formulas. This will automatically extend all column widths which reverses when pressed again.
Ctrl +'	Duplicate formula from cell above
F3	Paste named range in formula
Ctrl + Backspace	When navigated away while editing formula; jump back to active cell while keeping formula intact

Exhibit: Formulas – Trace Dependents and Precedents

Ctrl + [	Select direct precedents
Ctrl + Shift + {	Select all precedents
Ctrl +]	Select direct dependents
Ctrl + Shift +]	Select all dependents

Exhibit: Formulas – Manual Calculation

F9	Calculate all worksheets in all open workbooks
Shift + F9	Calculate the active worksheet
Ctrl + Alt + F9	Calculate all worksheets in all open workbooks, regardless of whether they have changed since the last calculation
Ctrl + Alt + Shift + F9	Recheck dependent formulas, and then calculates all cells in all workbooks, including cells not marked as needing to be calculated

Exhibit: Auto Filter

Ctrl + Shift + L	Turn AutoFilter on or off
Alt + Arrow Down	On the field with column head, display the AutoFilter list for the current column. Press Escape to cancel.
Alt + Arrow Up	Close the AutoFilter list for the current column

Home / End	Select the first item / last item in the AutoFilter list

Exhibit: Pivot Tables

Alt + NV	Insert PivotTable after selecting data range
F10 + R	Refresh PivotTable
Ctrl + -	Hide selected item
Alt + Arrow Down in header	Unhide item(s) by opening header drop-down and using Arrow Keys and Space to unhide item
Ctrl + Shift + *	Select the entire PivotTable report
Alt + Shift + Arrow Right	Group selected PivotTable items
Alt + Shift + Arrow Left	Ungroup selected PivotTable items when on group
Alt + JT X	Expand all fields
Alt + JT P	Collapse all fields
Ctrl + Shift + +	Insert pivot formula/ calculated field
Alt + F1	Create Pivot Chart in same Worksheet
F1	Create Pivot Chart in new Worksheet

IBM SPSS

AUTHOR BIO

Havish Madhvapaty

Havish presently works as Head of Research with Traverse Strategy Consultants, a research and consulting start-up, where he leads a team of analysts, spearheading research work. He is a corporate and academic trainer in quantitative analysis, focusing on Advanced Microsoft Excel and SPSS. He has trained organizations such as Uber, ITC, Tata Motors, WIPRO and so on. He is active on the Microsoft community as an expert contributor. Havish has over 25 academic publications in national and international journals, and has acted as a reviewer for IGI Global. He is pursuing his Ph.D. in the area of experiential marketing. He has authored a book titled RENVOI: Business Management Cases. His research assignments have been featured regularly in BW|Businessworld, BW|Applause, BW|Education, IMPACT and so on.

Is this chapter for you?

The chapter is designed for users who want to use SPSS software for statistical calculations. It gives easy to understand steps for the most commonly used graphs and analysis. The book caters to two groups: students who are insterested to use SPSS and professionals who use SPSS for data analysis.

Software Versions

The chapter is written for SPSS 21.0 for Windows. Users of other versions will also be able to follow all the steps as nearly all the information applies to other versions as well. The software is available in several forms – single user, multiuser, client-server, student version and so on.

Conventions

Tabs consist of commands.
Example: Help » Topics

1. INTRODUCTION TO SPSS

IBM SPSS statistics is a software that takes in raw data and combines them into new statistics, which is then used as predictors. The original software system named Statistical Package for Social Sciences (SPSS) was developed by Norman H. Nie, C. Hadlai (Tex) Hull, and Dale H. Bent. They developed the software to analyze large volumes of social science data, but then the package caught the interest of others at universities, and spread across universities, then to the government, and eventually to private enterprises. In 2008 the name was briefly changed to Predictive Analysis Software (PASW). SPSS Inc. was acquired by IBM in 2009 and the name changed to SPSS. It is known today as the official name IBM SPSS Statistics.

The following interfaces are available to perform SPSS functions:

a) **GUI (graphic user interface):** This is a windowing interface where commands are issued by using the mouse to make menu selections that cause dialog boxes to appear. This is the preferred interface for beginners.

b) **Syntax:** This is the internal language used to command actions, and is the command syntax of SPSS.

c) **Python:** This is a general-purpose language that has a collection of SPSS modules written for it. It can be used to write programs that work inside SPSS. The Syntax language can also be used to run Python to command SPSS to perform statistical functions. It is a modern and general-purpose language and offers several advantages such as ability to read and write data in other applications and in files.

d) **Scripts:** These are programs written in BASIC. It is a simple language and easy to use.

A. HOW IT WORKS

Variables are defined first, and then data is entered for the variables to create a number of *cases*. Each variable is a specific type such as *scale* for numeric measurement and *categorical* for defining categories. Once all cases are defined by values stored in the variables, analysis can be run. Graphs and charts can also be prepared. All output goes into the SPSS Viewer dialog box.

Input data and statistics are stored in files which can be of different types, containing numbers, definitions of numbers, graphics and so on.

B. HELP OPTIONS

There are various options to get help from within the software:

a) **Topics:** Choose Help » Topics from the main window. Choose Contents to select a heading from an extensive table of contents, choose Index to search for a heading by entering its name, or choose Search to enter a string search inside the body of the help text.

b) **Tutorial:** Choose Help » Tutorial. This opens a dialog box with the outline of a tutorial. There are various lessons available across sections.

c) **Case Studies:** Choose Help » Case Studies. The dialog box contains examples. Outlines contain titles with descriptions and examples.

d) **Statistics Coach:** Choose Help » Statistics Coach. This is useful when specific information is required for a particular topic.

e) **Command Syntax Reference:** Choose Help » Command Syntax Reference. A PDF viewer displays more than 1000 pages of references to the Syntax language. The document is much more detailed than regular help topics.

f) **Algorithms:** Choose Help » Algorithms. This shows detailed information on how processes work internally.

c. File Compatibility

SPSS recognizes the following formats:

a) IBM SPSS Statistics (.sav): IBM SPSS Statistics data, and also the format used by the DOS program SPSS/PC+.

b) dBase (.dbf): An interactive database system.

c) Excel (.xls): Spreadsheet for performing calculations on numbers in a grid.

d) Portable (.por): A portable format read and written by other versions of SPSS, including other operating systems.

e) Lotus (.w): Spreadsheet for performing calculations with numbers in a grid.

f) SAS (.sas7bdat, .sdy, .sd2, .ssd, and .xpt): Statistical analysis software.

g) Stata (.dta): Statistical analysis and graphics software.

h) Sylk (.slk): A symbolic link file format for transporting data from one application to another.

i) Systat (.syd and .sys): Software that produces statistical and graphical results.

d. Data Output

The output can be of the following file types:

a) Plain text

b) Unicode (UTF8 or UTF16)

c) HTML Web page

d) Excel file

e) Rich text format (RTF), readable by Word

f) PowerPoint display file

g) Portable document format (PDF)

Graphics can be output in the following formats:

a) Standard jpeg (JPG)
b) Portable network graphics (PNG)
c) Postscript (EPS)
d) Tagged image file format (TIFF)
e) Windows bitmap (BMP)
f) Enhanced metafile (EMF)

2. ENTERING DATA: AN EXAMPLE

The various *variables* viz. names, labels and data types need to be defined. The steps are:

a) Start SPSS. Depending on the way the software is configured, an options window might appear with OK and Cancel buttons. If so, click the Cancel button. The Data Editor window will appear.
b) Click on Variable View. This window allows us to define the names and types of variables, while the Data View window allows us to enter the values for those variables.
c) Type the following entries in the Name column:
    *   Year
    *   Month
    *   Day
    *   Hour
    *   Minute

Every field has both a name and a label. This is used as an identifier tag when data is displayed. The name is usually shorter than the label, which is intended to be more descriptive.

d) Skip the Type column. Since all fields are numeric, SPSS correctly guesses the attributes and fills them.
e) Set all values in Decimals column to zero.
f) Set the first value in Width column to 4 and rest of the values to 2. The year is set to 4 to accommodate 4 digits.
g) Type the following into cells in the Label column:
    *   Year of the show
    *   Number of the month
    *   Day of the month
    *   Hour of the day
    *   Minute of the hour
h) Skip the Values column, which is used for assigning names to specific values.
i) The Missing column is used to specify whether it is okay to have values missing from this field. The default is None as SPSS does not allow for missing data.
j) Skip the Columns column. The default is 8. It should be ensured that columns are big enough to hold largest data item or name.

k) Specify the alignment of data in the Align column. This is as per preference, and can be right, center, or left.

l) The Measure column can be set to Scale (default), Ordinal, or Nominal. For now, leave it to Scale.

m) Skip the Role column. For now, the Role of all variables in this example is standard: they hold input data. They could also be tagged as Target (or output) data, or as Both, or as None. A variable can be also designated as Partition and used to divide the data into separate samples.

n) Enter some random data as dates in Data View in the following format: 22/10/2014, 13:06

The Mean Hour

To find the mean of all hours (ignoring minutes), the steps are:

a) Choose Analyze » Descriptive Statistics » Descriptives.

b) Select hour of the day in the box on the left and click the arrow button in the middle of the window. The label moves to the right.

c) Click Options.

d) Select Mean, Std Deviation, Minimum, Maximum, Skewness and Kurtosis check boxes, and click Continue, then OK.

e) The SPSS Statistics Viewer appears and displays the results and information about the analysis.

f) The text on the far left shows the label given to the variable. The column labelled N is the number of data items included in the calculations. The minimum and maximum value is shown, as well as the value for the standard deviation is calculated according to the degree of variation from a perfect fit on a bell curve. Skewness represents the symmetry of the data A positive skewness indicates that more of the data appears to the high end, or the right, on the graph. A negative value indicates a skew to the lower values. Kurtosis refers to the flatness of the curve. If the data implies a curve flatter than the bell curve, the kurtosis value is negative. If the data inscribes a curve that is more pointed on top than the bell curve, the kurtosis value is positive.

Transforming Data

SPSS can combine hours and minutes fields into a new field that contains both. The steps are:

a) Choose Transform » Date and Time Wizard.

b) Select the option Create a Date / Time Variable from Variables Holding Parts of Dates or Times, and click Next.

c) Put names of variables in the appropriate fields. Only transfer hours and minutes, ignoring the rest, and click Next.

d)   Enter a name and a label for the variable, and select a display format from the list. Type **time** in the Result variable box, type **hour and minute** in the Variable Label box, and select **hh:mm** in the Output Format list.

e)   Select the Create the Variable Now option, and click the Finish button. This creates a new time data field.

Continuous vs. Categorical

The example data has used continuous variables, which are used for amounts and distances, such as age, number of students etc. Categorical variables represent each value as a category. All variables except the month number are continuous variables. To use month names instead of month number, the steps are:

a)   Click Variable View tab in Data Editor window, and select the cell in the Values column of the variable holding the month values.

b)   Click the button appearing in the cell.

c)   Enter a value and an associated name for each possible value, and click Add.

d)   The value and identifier is shown in the list below. Once all values are added, click OK.

e)   Choose Graphs » Legacy Dialogs » Pie.

f)   Select the Summaries for Groups of Cases option, and click Define.

g)   In the column on the left, select **number of the month**, and click the arrow to the left of Define Slices By. Then click OK.

Frequency of Day

a)   Choose Graphs » Legacy Dialogs » Bar.

b)   Select Simple Bar Chart and Summaries for Groups of Cases option, and click Define.

c)   For Bars Represent, select N of cases. Set Category Axis to the day of the month (day) and set Rows to be the number of the month (month).

d)   Click OK. The resulting charts shows distribution of days.

3. ENTERING DATA

SPSS can read data from other places, but data is usually entered manually, which also offers the maximum precision.

Data is organized into cases, which are made up of a collection of variables. After defining the characteristics of the variables that make up a case, data is entered into the variables to make up the contents of the cases.

Data is entered into the Variable View. There is a predefined set of 12 characteristics that specify all attributes of any variable. SPSS shows reasonable defaults as characteristics are entered.

A. OPTIONS

The various variable characteristics are:

a) **Name:** This is a short descriptor. It does not accept blanks.
b) **Type:** Other than numbers, the following special types can be defined:
   - Numeric – Standard numbers without decimal points.
   - Comma – Numeric values with commas inserted between three-digit groups. The format includes a period as a decimal point.
   - Dot – Same as Comma, except a period character (.) is used to group the digits into threes, and a comma is used for the decimal point.
   - Scientific Notation – A numeric variable that always includes the E to designate the power-of-ten exponent. The base, which is the part of the number to the left of the E, may or may not contain a decimal point. The exponent, which is the part of the number to the right of the E – which also may or may not contain a decimal – indicates how many times 10 multiplies itself, after which it is multiplied by the base to produce the actual number.
   - Date – Includes the year, month, day, hour, minute, and second.
   - Dollar – Shows a leading dollar sign and a period for a decimal point.
   - Custom Currency – Offers five custom currency formats.
   - String – Is non-numeric. Not used in calculations.
   - Width – Determines the number of characters used to display the value.
c) **Decimals:** Refers to the number of digits that appear to the right of the decimal point when the value appears on-screen.
d) **Label:** This is a long descriptor.
e) **Value:** Used to assign labels to all possible values of a variable.
f) **Missing:** Specifies what is to be entered for value that is missing for a variable in a case.
g) **Columns:** Specifies the width of the column used to enter data.
h) **Align:** Determines the position of the data in its allocated space, which could be left-aligned, right-aligned or center-aligned.
i) **Measure:** Specifies the measure of something as:
   - Scale – Number specifying magnitude. Most numbers fall in this category.
   - Ordinal – Number specifying position (order) in a list.
   - Nominal – Number specifying categories or types.
j) **Role:** Need not be used by most users. Specifies role assumed by variable. Options are:
   - Input – This is the default, used for input.
   - Target – Used as output by SPSS procedures.
   - Both – Used as both input and output.
   - None – Has no role assignment.
   - Partition – Used to partition the data into separate samples for training, testing, and validation.
   - Split – Used for round-trip compatibility with the SPSS modeler.

B. RECODING VARIABLES

SPSS can change values to other specific values based on rules that we specify.

a) Recoding into same variables:
- Choose Transform » Recode into Same Variables.
- Select the response variable and click the button with the arrow to move the variable to the panel on the right, labelled Numeric Variables
- Click the Old and New Values button. Enter an existing value in one of the Old Value choices, and then enter a New Value for it.
- Click Continue, then OK.

b) Recoding into same variables:
- Choose Transform » Recode into Different Variables.
- In the left panel, select the variable holding the values to be changed, and use the arrow in the center to move the variable name to the panel in the center.
- On the right, in the Output Variable area, enter a name and label for a new variable.
- Click Change.
- Click the Old and New Values button.
- Define the recoding.
- Click Continue, then OK.

c) Automatic recoding:
- Choose Transform » Automatic Recode.
- In the left panel, select the variable to be recoded, and use the arrow in the middle to move the variable to the panel on the right.
- Enter the name of the variable to receive the recoded values in the New Name text box.
- Click the Add New Name button, then OK.

4. GRAPHING DATA

SPSS can display data in various forms- such as a bar chart, line graph, area graph, pie chart, scatterplot, histogram, box plot and so on. Each of these basic forms can have multiple appearances, offering a large choice of layouts. *Chart* and *graph* mean the same in SPSS and are used interchangeably. There are three methods of creating a chart:

- Chart Builder
- Graphboard Template Choose
- Legacy Dialogs

A. ELEMENTS PROPERTIES DIALOG BOX

This dialog box is used to set properties of individual elements in a chart. The various possible options are:

a) **Edit Properties Of:** Used to select the element in the chart which needs to be edited. Each element has a type, which determines the other options available in the window.

b) **X:** Clicking the button removes the element from the list and from the graph.

c) **Arrow:** Arrow to the right indicates the variables that will be drawn on top of the other for charts with dual Y-axis variables.

d) **Statistics:** Statistics can be specified for certain elements. There are 32 statistic types available, such as Sum, Median, Variance and so on.

e) **Axis Label:** Refers to the text that describes a variable. The variable's label is default.

f) **Automatic:** The default automatically determines the range of the selected axis to display all values of variable along the axis.

g) **Minimum / Maximum:** Custom starting and ending points can be defined to replace automatic default values.

h) **Origin:** Specifies a point from which chart information is graphed.

i) **Major Increment:** Determines the spacing of placing of tick marks on an axis.

j) **Scale Type:** Four different types of scale can be used:
    - Linear – ruler-like scale.
    - Logarithmic (standard) – transforms values into logarithmic values.
    - Logarithmic (safe) – transforms values into logarithmic values; formulas can handle 0 and negative numbers.
    - Power – raises values to an exponential power.

k) **Sort By:** Defines the characteristic of a variable that will be used as a sort key. There are three options:
    - Label – Nominal variables are sorted in ascending or descending order by the names assigned to values.
    - Value – Numeric values are used for sorting in ascending or descending order.
    - Custom – Order specified in Order List is used.

l) **Order List:** Sorting order can be moved up or down the list by selecting a value and then clicking an arrow.

m) **Excluded:** Shows the values excluded from the Order List.

n) **Collapse:** Used to gather values that seldom occur.

o) **Error Bars:** Displays confidence intervals for Mean, Median, Count and Percentage.

p) **Bar Style:** Changes appearance of bars on a bar graph.

q) **Categories:** Defines the order (ascending or descending) in which values appear when placed on an axis.

r) **Small / Empty Categories:** Choose to include or exclude missing value information.

s) **Display Normal Curve:** A normal curve is superimposed over the chart, using the same mean and standard deviation as the histogram.

t) **Stack Identical Values:** Used for a dot plot chart. Defines whether points at the same location should appear next to each other or one on top of the other.

u) **Display Vertical Drop Lines between Points:** Shows a vertical line joining points with the same X-axis values for a dot plot chart.

v) **Plot Shape:** Three options are available for a dot plot:
   • Asymmetric – Default option which stacks the points on the X-axis.
   • Symmetric – Stacks the points centred around a line drawn horizontally across the center of the screen.
   • Flat – Same as Symmetric without a line drawn.

w) **Interpolation:** Defines the algorithm used to calculate the line drawn between points for line and area charts.

x) **Anchor Bin:** For histograms, defines the starting point of the first bin.

y) **Bin Sizes:** For histograms, defines sizes of bins.

z) **Angle:** Specify the clock position for first value by rotating a pie chart. Clockwise or counter clockwise inclusion is also defined.

aa) **Display Axis:** Displays the axis points on the outer rim for a pie chart.

B. SIMPLE LINE CHARTS

a) Choose Graphs » Chart Builder.
b) Select Line from Choose From list.
c) Drag first diagram to panel at the top.
d) In Variables list, drag first variable to Y-Axis rectangle in the panel at the top.
e) In Variables list, drag second variable to X-Axis rectangle in the panel at the top.
f) Click OK.

C. CHARTS WITH MULTIPLE LINES

a) Choose Graphs » Chart Builder.
b) Select Line from Choose From list.
c) Drag second diagram to panel at the top.
d) In Variables list, drag first variable to X-Axis rectangle in the panel at the top.
e) In Variables list, drag second variable to Y-Axis rectangle in the panel.
f) In Variables list, drag third variable to Y-Axis rectangle in the panel. Add this to the little box containing the plus sign.
g) Click OK.

D. SIMPLE SCATTERPLOTS

a) Choose Graphs » Chart Builder.
b) Select Scatter / Dot from Choose From list.
c) Drag the simplest scatterplot diagram to panel at the top.
d) In Variables list, drag first variable to X-Axis rectangle in the panel.

e)   In Variables list, drag second variable to Y-Axis rectangle in the panel.

f)   Click OK.

E. Scatterplots with Multiple Variables

a)   Choose Graphs » Chart Builder.

b)   Select Line from Choose From list.

c)   Drag second scatterplot diagram to panel at the top.

d)   In Variables list, drag first variable to X-Axis rectangle in the panel at the top.

e)   In Variables list, drag second variable to Y-Axis rectangle in the panel.

f)   In Variables list, drag third variable to Y-Axis rectangle in the panel. Add this to the little box containing the plus sign.

g)   Click OK.

F. Simple Three-Dimensional Scatterplots

a)   Choose Graphs » Chart Builder.

b)   Select Scatter / Dot from Choose From list.

c)   Drag third scatterplot diagram to panel at the top.

d)   In Variables list, drag first variable to X-Axis rectangle in the panel at the top.

e)   In Variables list, drag second variable to Y-Axis rectangle in the panel.

f)   In Variables list, drag third variable to Z-Axis rectangle in the panel.

g)   Click OK.

G. Grouped Three-Dimensional Scatterplots

a)   Choose Graphs » Chart Builder.

b)   Select Scatter / Dot from Choose From list.

c)   Drag fourth scatterplot diagram to panel at the top.

d)   In Variables list, drag first variable to Z-Axis rectangle in the panel at the top.

e)   In Variables list, drag second variable to Y-Axis rectangle in the panel.

f)   In Variables list, drag third variable to Y-Axis rectangle in the panel. Add this to the little box containing the plus sign.

g)   Drag INDEX from X-Axis rectangle to the Set Color rectangle at the upper right.

h)   In Variables list, drag fourth variable to X-Axis rectangle in the panel

i)   Click OK.

H. Grouped Three-Dimensional Scatterplots

a)   Choose Graphs » Chart Builder.

b)   Select Scatter / Dot from Choose From list.

c)   Drag fifth scatterplot diagram to panel at the top.

d)   In Variables list, drag first variable to X-Axis rectangle in the panel at the top.

e)   In Variables list, drag second variable to Y-Axis rectangle in the panel.

f) In Variables list, drag third variable to Y-Axis rectangle in the panel. Add this to the little box containing the plus sign.

g) Click OK.

I. SIMPLE DOT PLOTS

a) Choose Graphs » Chart Builder.
b) Select Scatter / Dot from Choose From list.
c) Drag sixth graph image to panel at the top.
d) In Variables list, drag the variable to X-Axis rectangle in the panel at the top.
e) Click OK.

J. SCATTERPLOT MATRICES

a) Choose Graphs » Chart Builder.
b) Select Scatter / Dot from Choose From list.
c) Drag seventh graph image to panel at the top.
d) In Variables list, drag the first variable to the Scattermatrix rectangle in the panel at the top.
e) Drag the other variable names to the rectangle inside the panel at the top of the window.
f) Click OK.

K. DROP-LINE CHARTS

a) Choose Graphs » Chart Builder.
b) Select Scatter / Dot from Choose From list.
c) Drag last graph image to panel at the top.
d) In Variables list, drag first variable to the rectangle in the upper-right corner with the Set Color label.
e) In Variables list, drag second variable to X-Axis rectangle in the panel.
f) In Variables list, drag third variable to the rectangle on the left labelled Mean.
g) Click OK.

L. SIMPLE BAR GRAPHS

a) Choose Graphs » Chart Builder.
b) Select Bar from Choose From list.
c) Drag first graph image to panel at the top.
d) In Variables list, drag first variable to X-Axis rectangle.
e) In Variables list, drag second variable to the Count rectangle.
f) Click OK.

M. Clustered Bar Charts

a) Choose Graphs » Chart Builder.
b) Select Bar from Choose From list.
c) Drag second graph image to panel at the top.
d) In Variables list, drag first variable to X-Axis rectangle.
e) In Variables list, drag second variable to the Count rectangle.
f) In Variables list, drag third variable to rectangle in the upper-right corner. This would be labelled Cluster on X.
g) Click OK.

N. Stacked Bar Charts

a) Choose Graphs » Chart Builder.
b) Select Bar from Choose From list.
c) Drag third graph image to panel at the top.
d) In Variables list, drag first variable to X-Axis rectangle.
e) In Variables list, drag second variable to the Count rectangle.
f) In Variables list, drag third variable to the rectangle in the upper-right corner. This would be labelled Stack.
g) Click OK.

O. Simple Error Bars

a) Choose Graphs » Chart Builder.
b) Select Bar from Choose From list.
c) Drag seventh graph image to panel at the top.
d) In Element Properties window, check the Display Error Bars option and Confidence Intervals option. Set the level to 95%
e) In Variables list, drag first variable to the X-axis rectangle.
f) In Variables list, drag second variable to Mean rectangle.
g) Click OK.

P. Clustered Error Bars

a) Choose Graphs » Chart Builder.
b) Select Bar from Choose From list.
c) Drag eighth graph image to panel at the top.
d) In Variables list, drag first variable to the X-axis rectangle.
e) In Variables list, drag second variable to Mean rectangle.
f) In Variables list, drag third variable to the upper-right corner. This would be labelled Cluster on X.
g) Click OK.

Q. SIMPLE HISTOGRAMS

a) Choose Graphs » Chart Builder.
b) Select Histogram from Choose From list.
c) Drag first graph diagram to panel at the top.
d) In Variables list, drag first variable to the X-axis rectangle.
e) In Variables list, drag second variable to the Count rectangle on left side of the panel.
f) Click OK.

R. STACKED HISTOGRAMS

a) Choose Graphs » Chart Builder.
b) Select Histogram from Choose From list.
c) Drag second graph diagram to panel at the top.
d) In Variables list, drag first variable to the X-axis rectangle.
e) In Variables list, drag second variable to the Count rectangle on left side of the panel.
f) In Variables list, drag third variable to the Stack Set Color rectangle at upper right.
g) Click OK.

S. FREQUENCY POLYGONS

a) Choose Graphs » Chart Builder.
b) Select Histogram from Choose From list.
c) Drag third graph diagram to panel at the top.
d) In Variables list, drag first variable to the X-axis rectangle.
e) In Variables list, drag second variable to the Mean rectangle.
f) Click OK.

T. POPULATION PYRAMIDS

a) Choose Graphs » Chart Builder.
b) Select Histogram from Choose From list.
c) Drag fourth graph diagram to panel at the top.
d) In Variables list, drag first variable to the Split Variable rectangle.
e) In Variables list, drag second variable to the Distribution Variable rectangle.
f) Click OK.

U. SIMPLE AREA GRAPHS

a) Choose Graphs » Chart Builder.
b) Select Area from Choose From list.
c) Drag first graph diagram to panel at the top.
d) In Variables list, drag first variable to the X-Axis rectangle.

e) In Variables list, drag second variable to the Count rectangle.
f) Click OK.

v. STACKED AREA CHARTS

a) Choose Graphs » Chart Builder.
b) Select Area from Choose From list.
c) Drag second graph diagram to panel at the top.
d) In Variables list, drag first variable to the X-Axis rectangle.
e) In Variables list, drag second variable to the Count rectangle.
f) In Variables list, drag third variable to the plus sign in the second variable rectangle.
g) Click OK.

w. PIE CHARTS

a) Choose Graphs » Chart Builder.
b) Select Pie / Polar from Choose From list.
c) Drag pie diagram to panel at the top.
d) In Variables list, drag first variable to the Slice By rectangle at bottom of the panel.
e) Click OK.

x. SIMPLE BOXPLOTS

a) Choose Graphs » Chart Builder.
b) Select Boxplot from Choose From list.
c) Drag first graph diagram to panel at the top.
d) In Variables list, drag first variable to the X-Axis rectangle.
e) In Variables list, drag second variable to the Y-Axis rectangle.
f) Click OK.

y. CLUSTERED BOXPLOTS

a) Choose Graphs » Chart Builder.
b) Select Boxplot from Choose From list.
c) Drag second graph diagram to panel at the top.
d) In Variables list, drag first variable to the X-Axis rectangle.
e) In Variables list, drag second variable to the Y-Axis rectangle.
f) In Variables list, drag third variable to the Cluster on X rectangle.
g) Click OK.

z. DIFFERENCED AREA GRAPHS

a) Choose Graphs » Chart Builder.

b)   Select High-Low from Choose From list.
c)   Drag fourth graph diagram to panel at the top.
d)   In Variables list, drag first variable to the X-Axis rectangle.
e)   In Variables list, drag second variable to the Y-Axis rectangle.
f)   In Variables list, drag third variable to the other Y-Axis rectangle.
g)   Click OK.

aa. Dual Y-Axes with Categorical X-Axis

a)   Choose Graphs » Chart Builder.
b)   Select Dual Axes from Choose From list.
c)   Drag first diagram to panel at the top.
d)   In Variables list, drag first variable to the Y-Axis rectangle on the left.
e)   In Variables list, drag second variable to the Y-Axis rectangle on the right. This
     would be named Count.
f)   In Variables list, drag third variable to the other X-Axis rectangle.
g)   Click OK.

5. ANALYSIS

SPSS offers both basic and advanced form of analysis. The advanced forms employ the same basic algorithms, but require setting up of more options.

a. Comparison of Means Analyses

a) Simple Means Compare

A simple comparison table can be generated by choosing Analyze » Compare Means » Means. A dialog box will appear showing a list of variable names on the left. Select the variables to be used for calculating the mean and transfer them to the Dependent List panel by using the arrow button.

The table produced will show the means, a count of number of cases, and the standard deviation by default. More options can be accessed by clicking on the Options button. There are 21 statistics available.

b) One-Sample T Test

This test compares an expected value with a mean derived from the values of a single variable. Choose Analyze » Compare Means » One Sample T Test.

The first column labelled with the letter t is the mean value derived from the data. The second column labelled df is the degrees of freedom. The Mean Difference column is the average of the magnitude of the differences between the values and the expected value. The Confidence Interval values show how wide the range is around the value to include 95 percent of all values.

c) Independent-Sample T Test

This test compares the means of two sets of values from one variable. Choose Analyze » Compare Means » Independent-Samples T Test.

One variable is moved to the Test Variable(s) panel, which supplies the value for the means we want to test. The other variable is moved to the Grouping Variable panel, and is used to select the two groups.

The Independent Samples Test table displays the two means, the standard deviation and standard error for the two means. Further information is provided on the mean in two rows of numbers. The decision to use the row for equal variances or the one for unequal variances is taken on the basis of the following:

- If the significance of the Levene test is high (greater than 0.05), the values in the first row are applicable.
- If the significance of the Levene test is low, the numbers in the second row are more applicable.
- If the two-tailed significance of the is low, it indicates a significant difference in the two means.
- If none of the numbers of the 95 percent confidence interval are 0, it indicates that the difference between the means is significant.

d) Paired-Sample T Test

This is a comparison test designed to compare values from the same group at different times. Choose Analyze » Compare Means » Paired-Samples T Test.

The double-headed arrow in the dialog box can be used to swap variable 1 and variable 2 in any pair.

e) One-Way ANOVA

ANOVA is an acronym for Analysis of Variance. A one-way ANOVA analyses the variance of values of a dependent variable by comparing them against another set of values of the independent variable. The test of hypothesis is that the mean of the tested variable is equal to that of the factor.

B. CORRELATION ANALYSES

These tests determine the similarity or difference in the way two variables change in value through the data.

a) Bivariate

Choose Analyze » Correlate » Bivariate. There are three types of correlation. Pearson correlation is the default. Options button can be used to define treatment of missing values and choose preference to calculate standard deviations.

Correlation figures vary from -1 to +1.

b) Partial correlation

Partial correlation accounts for outside factors that affect a correlation. Choose Analyze » Correlate » Partial.

c. REGRESSION ANALYSES

Regression analysis is used for predicting the future based on past data collected. A mathematical equation is determined which forecasts within a certain range of probability. One independent variable is used for *simple regression* and more than one independent variable for *multiple regression*.

a) Linear

Is used when projections are expected to be in a straight line with actual values. Choose Analyze » Regression » Linear.

b) Curve Estimation

This is non-linear regression. A curve is constructed that passes through (or near) a collection of data points. Interpolation draws a curve that connects the existing points and extrapolation extends the curve beyond the existing points. Choose Analyze » Regression » Curve Estimation.

There are three options available as the types of curves:

- Linear
- Quadratic
- Cubic

6. CONCLUSION

SPSS started specifically for social sciences, but areas such as marketing, finance, HR etc. have also found immense use for it. It is extensively used by market researchers, survey companies, analysts, students, government, organizations etc. Advanced users can use SPSS Modeler, which enables building predictive models.

Data mining and text analytics can also be performed. SPSS AMOS is a powerful structural equation modelling software that extends standard SPSS multivariate analysis methods, and is used to build attitudinal and behavioural models that reflect complex relationships more accurately.

R (PROGRAMMING LANGUAGE)

AUTHOR BIO

Vipul Pandey

Vipul presently works as Business Analyst for a leading product based IT company. He has done his MBA in Marketing and Information Technology and Bachelors in Computer Science Engineering. He extensively used analytics for the website portal Vidyashala.in, which he also co-founded. Vipul also has rich development experience with leading IT-MNC in Java- J2EE and Struts.

1. INTRODUCTION TO R

R is a statistical programming language which is widely used in industry and academia for statistical analysis and data visualization. R has emerged as a powerful open-source tool to perform statistical operations on any data-set. Although R as a programming language is the contribution of several programmers across the world, initially it was written by Robert Gentleman and Ross Ihaka (Contributors: R Foundation).

A simple search for R-programming jobs in India reveals 116894 jobs listed in Naukri.com[1]. R language is simple to learn but there are certain perquisites for understanding R in a better way, some of which are:

a)   Elementary knowledge of statistics.
b)   Elementary knowledge of any programming language and its constructs or knowhow of basics of any scripting language is recommended.

These are required as this chapter aims at imparting skills to start with R programming and to interpret the data. The chapter is intended for beginners of R language and is not meant for advanced R users or practitioners. The chapter provides an introductory level overview on using R programming language in data analysis and visualization. According to a report by Gartner, R is being used by more than 50% of data science teams in some capacity and is constantly penetrating business intelligence community. The low-cost alternative that R language has as compared to traditional premium data science tools is considered as its advantage point.

A. INSTALLING R

The latest version of Java must be installed before installing R else running any script will give an *Error* like
"No CurrentVersion entry in Software/JavaSoft registry! Try re-installing Java and make sure R and Java have matching architectures".

R is an open source platform and can be installed easily by going to official R foundation website and using this link
https://cloud.r-project.org.

Here one can get links for various operating systems like Mac OS, Windows, Linux and download the appropriate version of R. One can download R for Windows (32/64 bit) from the link[2]. Once R is downloaded it can be run from the installation directory or desktop shortcut. After this installation, we need to install R-Studio which can be downloaded from the link.[3]

---

[1]   This data is taken from simple search result from Naukri.com as accessed on 18/2/2017 and is bound to change.

[2]   https://cloud.r-project.org/bin/windows/base/R-3.3.2-win.exe

[3]   https://www.rstudio.com/products/rstudio/download

The R 3.3.2 (Windows version) is used for the purpose of explanations and examples in this chapter. R-Studio gives an easy to use graphical user interface (GUI) which is like any other integrated development platform (IDE).

B. STARTING WITH R PROGRAMMING

The Exhibit shows the welcome screen of R Studio which would open once R is run.

a) Getting accustomed with the interface

The introductory screen as shown in the Exhibit is the R-console and it shows the output of any script or command written in R.

Exhibit: R Interface

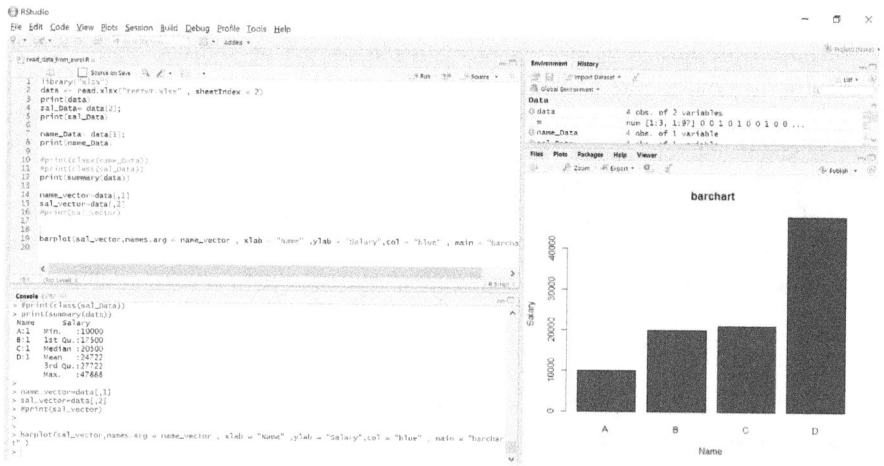

The different types of windows in R are:

a) **Console Window:** This is used to show the execution of commands in R and also displays the output of R scripts.

b) **Script Window:** This window is used to write any script or simply a program to write R code.

c) **Environment Window:** This window shows the variables that are initialized in the R script

d) **Plots Windows:** This window shows the graphs and plots for various analysis.

b) Variables and Data Types

A variable is used to store a value or a temporary memory location. Variables can be assigned in R in the following ways:

- Using equal operator

Data = 1   # Initialize the variable data1 with value 1

- Using leftward operator

Data <- 1   # Initialize the variable data1 with value 1

- Using outward operator

1 -> data   # Initialize the variable data1 with value 1

Please note that # represents comments in R, which will not be executed if written in the code.

The variables are not declared with some data types in R as with other programming language but assigned as R-Objects, and the variable takes the same data type of the R-Object.

Various types of R-Objects are Vectors, Matrices, Lists, Arrays, Factors and Data Frames.

c. EXAMPLES ON CREATING VARIOUS OBJECTS

a) Create a vector with different fruits

Code

```
vector_fruits <- c('grapes','apples','banana')
print(vector_fruits)
```

Output
[1] "grapes" "apples" "banana"

#Above code initializes the vector with different fruits, function c() is used to combine elements in one vector
#Note that variable name could refer to anything that supports naming convention.

b) Create a list with different elements

Code
```
list_elements = list(c(1,2,3), 'abc', sum(2,3))
print(list_elements)
```

Output
```
[[1]]
[1] 1 2 3

[[2]]
[1] "abc"

[[3]]
[1] 5
```

c) Create an array with different elements

Code
```
a <- array(c('green',1,4), dim = c(3,3))
print(a)
```

Output
```
[,1] [,2] [,3]
[1,] "green" "green" "green"
[2,] "1" "1" "1"
[3,] "4" "4" "4"
```

#dim() function is used to give dimensions of the array to be formed.

d) Create a data frame with different elements.

Code
```
BMI <-  data.frame(
gender = c("F", "M","F"),
height = c(120, 123.5, 133),
weight = c(71,53, 78),
Age = c(22,38,26)
)
print(BMI)
```

Output

	Gender	Height	Weight	Age
1	F	120.0	71	22
2	M	123.5	53	38
3	F	133.0	78	26

#Data Frame can be seen as the list of vectors containing different types of data.

e) Loops

Code
```
for(i in 1:10){
print(i)
}
```
Output
```
[1] 1
[1] 2
[1] 3
[1] 4
[1] 5
[1] 6
[1] 7
[1] 8
[1] 9
[1] 10
```

f) Conditional statement

Code
```
v1 = 1:10 # vector v1 initialized with values from 1 to 10
t = 3 # another variable t initialized with value 3
if (t %in% v1) {# checks whether vector v1 has value of 3
print(t+1)    # True condition
} else{
print('not available') # False condition
}
```
Output
```
[1] 4
```

D. READING DATA FROM EXCEL FILE

Excel sheet data in sheet2
Table 1
Output

Name	Salary	Percentage
A	10000	5%
B	20000	10%
C	21000	10%
D	47888	23%
E	10000	5%
F	50000	25%
G	25000	12%
H	20000	10%
Total	203888	100%

Code

```
install.packages("xlsx") # This is required if you do not have this package to use
library("xlsx")
data <- read.xlsx("testwt.xlsx", sheetIndex = 3)
print(data)
```

Output

```
Name Salary
1 A 10000
2 B 20000
3 C 21000
4 D 47888
```

Also in global environment window on the top right variable data has been created which consists of 3 observations and 2 variables in this case.

For large Excel files it is advisable to convert the file to CSV (Comma Separated File) to avoid long import time and memory issues.

Reading a CSV file
Code

```
data4 = read.csv("Sample_Data.csv")
print(data4)
```

E. ACCESSING COLUMNS

We have seen how to read data in R through Excel and csv file and store them into a variable. Specific columns and data values can also be accessed from this retrieved data set.

Let us say we have the following Exhibit as our data set.

Exhibit: Data Set

Respondent No.	S1. Age Group	S2. Country	S3. Providence
IRB15USB203920007	56 - 65	United States	Maine
IRB15USB203920010	Over 65	United States	Missouri
IRB15USB203920014	56 – 65	United States	Illinois
IRB15USB203920015	56 – 65	United States	South Carolina
IRB15USB203920017	56 – 65	United States	New Jersey
IRB15USB203920012	46 – 55	United States	Pennsylvania
IRB15USB203920021	46 – 55	United States	New York
IRB15USB203920023	36 – 45	United States	Kentucky
IRB15USB203920024	56 – 65	United States	Illinois
IRB15USB203920026	46 – 55	United States	Michigan
IRB15USB203920027	56 – 65	United States	Illinois
IRB15USB203920028	46 – 55	United States	New Jersey
IRB15USB203920029	56 – 65	United States	Wisconsin
IRB15USB203920030	Over 65	United States	New York

EXTRACTING ROW AND COLUMNS FROM THE DATA FRAME CREATED FROM THE ABOVE SAMPLE DATA

Code

```
data5 = read.csv("Sample_Data.csv")
class(data5)
result = data5[2:5,3:4]
print(result)
```

Output

S2. Country	S3. Providence
United States	Missouri
United States	Illinois

United States	South Carolina
United States	New Jersey

As shown in output, the given code extracts rows from 2 to 5 from our sample and columns from 3 to 4. Likewise the data frame argument d[1:10, 2:4] means that we need to extract rows 1 to 10 and columns 2 to 4 from any data frame.

F. FREQUENCY CALCULATION

Frequency of any categorical variable in the data set can be found using the following code.

Code
library(MASS)
test1=data5[1:14,4]
test1.freq=table(test1)
print(test1.freq)

The code will show the frequency of various cities in Providence column as per Table 2 sample data. To find all levels of data that is available for a given column, use $ sign with the data frame to address the field for which it is required.

Code
data5$S2..Country

Output
Levels: Canada United States

G. MEAN AND MEDIAN

Code
```
library("xlsx")
data2 <- read.xlsx("testwt.xlsx", sheetIndex = 2)
print(data2)
mean1= mean(data2$Salary)
print(mean1)
median1= median(data2$Salary)
print(median1)
```

Output
[1] 25486
[1] 20500

H. SIMPLE BAR CHART

R gives proper visualization of your data which can come in form of bar graphs. The following code creates a bar chart visualization for the data.

Code

```
library("xlsx")
data <- read.xlsx("testwt.xlsx", sheetIndex = 2)
name_vector = data[, 1] #data from column 1 is stored into name_vector variable
sal_vector = data[, 2]    #data from column 2 is stored into sal_vector variable
barplot(
sal_vector,
names.arg = name_vector,
xlab = "Name",
ylab = "Salary",
col = "blue",
main = "barchart"
)
```

Output

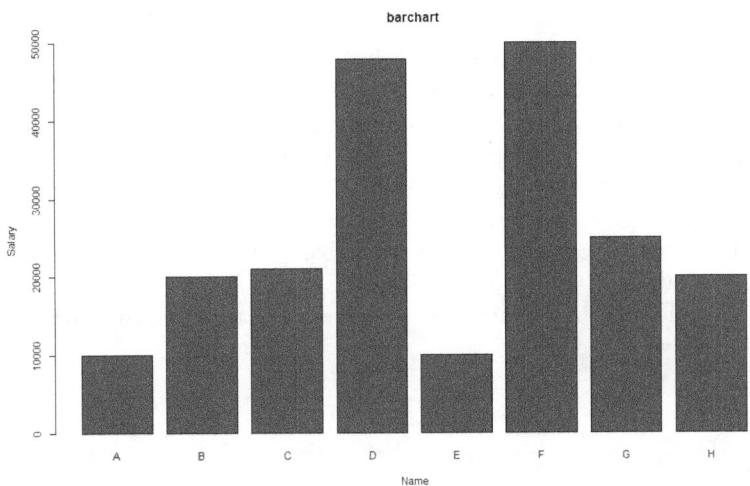

I. PIE-CHART

Code

```
percentage_vector = (data[1:4, 3]) *100
percentage_vector=trunc(percentage_vector, prec=2)
print(percentage_vector)
```

pie(percentage_vector, labels = percentage_vector, main = "Pie chart percentage salary ")

Output

Pie chart percenatage salary

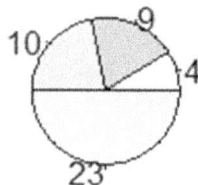

J. SENTIMENT ANALYSIS

R is a powerful tool that not only helps us to analyze data from structured database but could also be used for analyzing the user sentiments from the Tweets posted on various twitter handlers. This feature of R is extensively being used for analyzing customer feedback for service as well as product industries. In the era of social media, people use social media handlers and product review forums for posting the feedbacks. Imagine a scenario where thousands of tweets have to be analyzed to understand the root cause analysis of the problem or general satisfaction level of customers in real time.

This could be done by technique called sentiment analysis and could be handled by R using following code:

```
library(twitteR)
library(plyr)
library(RCurl)
library(ROAuth)
library(stringr)
reqURL <- "https://api.twitter.com/oauth/request_token"
accessURL <- "https://api.twitter.com/oauth/access_token"
authURL <- "https://api.twitter.com/oauth/authorize"
api_Key <- "Enter your key"
api_Secret <- "Enter your api_Secret"
access_token="Enter access token"
```

access_secret="Enter access secret"
setup_twitter_oauth(api_Key, api_Secret, access_token,access_secret)
tweets <- searchTwitter("@airtel_care", n=10) #n represents no. of tweets to retreive
tweets

Output

[[1]]
[1] "Indrajithonline: RT @airtel_care: @Indrajithonline Hello @Airtel_Presence, kindly assist with stated issue. Thank you. ^Osebi."

[[2]]
[1] "srikanthviru: @KSriniReddy @airtelindia Every @airtelindia users ############
[1] "puneet3210: @airtelindia @Airtel_Presence @airtel_care and please #########
[1] "puneet3210: @airtelindia @Airtel_Presence @airtel_care I' changes to plan. Please spare"##################

[[5]]
[1] "ekanemantia: @airtel_care how do I use#######
[[6]]
[1] "ekanemantia: @airtel_care pls I need to knw how

[[7]]
[1] "satsangi: Congratulations! @Airtel_Presence @airtelindia @a

[[8]]
[1] "Indrajithonline: RT @airtel_care: @Indrajithonline @Indrajithonline, Nice!! ^Ade"

[[9]]
[1] "iamtennygee: @airtel_care Thank you"

[[10]]
[1] "YatinBhatia431: @airtel_care @Airtel_Presence @airtel_care @airtelindia Am waiting for revert"

Please note that before you use the above code Twitter API should be setup by logging in with your credentials. After this basic data retrieval from the respective twitter handler, words could be analyzed with the help of various customized algorithms like matching them with certain set of positive and negative words stored in a file and determining the frequency for positive and negative feedback which could be used to understand the service level satisfaction of the user.

2. CONCLUSION

R's popularity has increased over the years, especially among data miners. R is also easily extensible through functions and extensions. The R community is also noted for its active contributions in terms of packages. Static graphics are another strength of, as it can produce production-quality graphics, including mathematical symbols. Dynamic and interactive graphics are available through additional packages. Major commercial software systems support connections to R.

ABOUT THE AUTHORS

Dr. Anupama Rajesh

Professor

Amity Business School, Amity University Uttar Pradesh, India

Dr. Anupama Rajesh is Professor at Amity Business School, Amity University, India. Her qualifications include Ph.D. in the area of Technology in Education, M.Phil. (IT), M.Phil. (Mgmt.), M.Ed., M.Sc. (IT), PGDCA, PGDBA. She has also been trained for Case Writing at INSEAD Paris. She has a teaching experience of about 20 years including international assignments which include a teaching stint in London and Singapore and training of Italian and French delegates and students. She has written more than 40 research papers and case studies for prestigious international journals and has eight books and several book chapters to her credit. She is reviewer of renowned Sage and Emerald journals. Her research interests are Business Intelligence, Educational Technology, Marketing Analytics etc. while her teaching interests are Business Intelligence, E-Commerce, IT enabled processes and so on.

She is an avid trainer and has trained Union Bank of India, NHPC, ILFS, TATA Motors, Bhutan Power Company employees as well as Commonwealth Games Volunteers and army personnel. She is a Master Trainer from Microsoft, Infosys Partner for Business Intelligence and Academic Partner for SAP ERM Sim.

She has recently won the ADMA Research Award and has also been awarded several Outstanding Paper Awards at prestigious conferences at institutes such as IIM Ahmedabad. She also has a MOOC to her credit.

Havish Madhvapaty

Head of Research & Analytics – Traverse Strategy Consultants

Havish has diverse experience across sales and marketing, academia and market research. He is a Ph.D. scholar researching experiential marketing. His qualifications include Microsoft certified **Microsoft Office Specialist (MOS) Master, Google Analytics & Google AdWords Certified** and **VSkills Certified Digital Marketing Master.** He has also been an MBA Gold Medallist and Scholarship Awardee.

Havish presently works as Head of Research & Analytics with Traverse Strategy Consultants, a research and consulting start-up, where he leads a team of analysts, spearheading research work. He has had the opportunity to work on significant projects for Government of India (Ministry of Tourism, Ministry of Finance, Ministry of Commerce etc.)

He is a corporate and academic trainer in quantitative analysis, focusing on Advanced Microsoft Excel and SPSS. He has trained organizations such as Uber, ITC, Tata Motors, S. Chand, WIPRO etc. In addition to Microsoft Excel, he is also proficient in MS PowerPoint, MS Word and MS Project. He is active on the Microsoft community as an expert contributor.

Havish has over 25 academic publications in national and international journals, and has acted as a reviewer for IGI Global. He has authored a book titled RENVOI: Business Management Cases. His research assignments have been featured regularly in BW|Businessworld, BW|Applause, BW|Education, IMPACT, Pitch; and on websites of Amagi, Businessworld, CMO.com, Colgate Palmolive, Goa Tourism, Indiantelevision, Marico, SEBI, Yahoo News and so on.

VATSAL SAHANI

Vatsal Sahani is currently pursuing his education from Mayo College, Ajmer (India) where he has secured a perfect 10 CGPA and was awarded a Special Medal for Excellence in Academics along with the Mayo College General Council Scholarship and Mahindra Search for Talent Scholarship for topping the batch. He has cleared the Advance Placements Exams (AP) with Honors and secured a 35 on the standardised ACT test placing him in the 99th percentile globally. Vatsal holds a B1 DELF certification from the Ministry of France where he cleared all the levels with high distinction.

He has represented Mayo at the World School Debates, Slovenia and has been an ambassador to Mayo both in India and abroad through his experiences at the Round Square International Conference in Singapore, and for football in World Sports Festival in Austria and the French Festival in Pakistan.

He is a certified Google Adword, Google Search, Google Analytics specialist and Microsoft Office Specialist (MOS) master who codes in C and C++. Additionally he is a certified Stock Market/MCX Research and Technical Analyst, and has work experience in the financial sector through his internship at Market Hub Stock Broking and in analytics at VRentin Tech Pvt. Ltd.

In 2017, he completed a project with the Harvard University South Asia Institute with recommendation and was accepted into the Young Leaders for Active Citizenship (YLAC) cohort.